D0930814

Perspectives on Scripture and Tradition

Essays in Honor of Dale Moody

edited by
Robert L. Perkins

MERCER
UNIVERSITY PRESS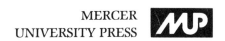

Wingate College Library

ISBN 0-86554-305-4

Perspectives on Scripture and Tradition
Copyright © 1987
Mercer University Press
Macon, Georgia 31207
All rights reserved
Printed in the United States of America

The paper used in this publication meets
the minimum requirements of American National Standard
for Information Sciences—Permanence of paper
for Printed Library Materials, ANSI Z39.48-1984.

CONTENTS

Editorial Introduction

Dale Moody, Christian Gentleman, scholar, teacher, preacher, controversialist, devoted husband and father, but always, first and last, a Christian Gentleman.

I used the word Christian twice in the above sentence, and I did not use the word Baptist at all. Let no one misunderstand; Dale Moody is a Baptist. But first he is a Christian, and then we may qualify and say that he is a Christian of the Baptist variety.

As anyone knows us at all can testify, Baptists are not all alike. Perhaps Dale Moody's greatest contribution to me was to show that we could hold different theological convictions in the community of Christ's love. Convictions, differences and unity in the bond of Christ. That was a liberating, though terrifying, thought when I was an illiterate nineteen year old. What an exciting night that was in Room 308 of Elizabeth Hall at Stetson University when Dale Moody gave my fundamentalist Scofield dispensationalism a thoroughly biblical thumping. That was neither the first nor the last time Moody "out-Bibled" an opponent. Vehement, to be sure. Prideful, arrogant, never.

Dale Moody was, is and, I pray, will always be a controversialist. I do not have to pray that he will be loving, courteous and liberal to those who differ with him. Those are fundamental qualities of his character. Dale Moody will expect you to convince him of error, or he will expect you to acknowledge the correctness of his position. When the final hermeneutical judgment has been made, he will respect and love those who still differ with him. May Dale Moody in the years remaining to him find his equals, if not in knowledge, at least may he find his equals in the love of God and neighbor and in the joy of the pursuit of theological truth.

I just used the word error and I have used the language of conviction liberally. Dale Moody, like his critics, believes in theology and in theological truth. Theology is not just opinions and vague, disorganized reflections for Dale Moody. Here he and his critics are one. Dale Moody has put his life and energy, and the energy is considerable, into being the best informed theological mind Southern Baptists have ever had. When he speaks, it is with the authority of knowledge, of having struggled with the whole theological tradition of Christianity, broadly conceived. Not one of his critics has an equivalent knowledge base from which to argue.

Perhaps nothing is so ironic to those of us who learned from him and who admired the teacher as the fact that this free, liberating biblical scholar, this learned man, has been hounded for his integrity and loyalty to his best insights into the Bible by the emergence of an arrogant and unexamined traditionalism and prideful dogmatism that will divide over differences rather than enjoy and rejoice in the differences we share. I am the last to admit that Dale Moody is correct in all his conclusions, but I rejoice in his learning, his convictions, his energy, his devotion to theology, his evangelistic zeal, his enormous preaching skills, his great heart, the freedom with which he is willing to engage in wrenching theological debate, his fairness in argument, his joy in the engaged search for truth, and his courage and willingness to take an unpopular theological position regardless of the cost—and the costs have been great. A man has moved among us. A Christian scholar has moved among us. A Christian Gentleman has witnessed to us of the love and majesty of God.

These essays salute and celebrate our great friend, our brother in Christ, our tenacious colleague in the vocation of Christian learning and teaching, and our fellow traveller to the City of God.

I wish to thank the contributors for their efforts. All of them sacrificed leisure with family, rest or both to bring this Festschrift to publication. Finally, I wish to thank the persons responsible for asking me to edit this volume. It has been a great privilege to express the honor in which I hold Dale Moody in this way.

Robert L. Perkins
Stetson University

DALE MOODY:
BIBLE TEACHER
EXTRAORDINAIRE

E. GLENN HINSON
THE SOUTHERN BAPTIST THEOLOGICAL SEMINARY
LOUISVILLE KY 40280

Sermons, classroom lectures, books, articles, research, conversation—they all tell one story: Dale Moody has sought to be and has been an extraordinary teacher and preacher of the Bible. If everyone understood what it meant, he would be just as happy with a B.T., for Bible Teacher, after his name as he has been with the B.A., Th.M., Th.D., and D.Phil. (Oxon.), all earned with distinction. For most of his career he has spent virtually every weekend teaching or preaching the Bible—the two differing only in time allotted, fifty minutes to teach, thirty to preach.

Sit in a pew and listen to him preach, and you will hear the message of the Bible leap out at you with grace and power, structured to be remembered, more often than not by way of alliteration in threes. When you hear Dale Moody, you will know the truth of Hebrews 4:12: ''For the word of God is living and active, sharper than any two-edged sword, piercing to the division of soul and spirit, of joints and marrow, and discerning the thoughts and intentions of the heart.''

Sit at a desk in his classroom, as thousands did at The Southern Baptist Theological Seminary where he taught for forty-one years, and you will again find a Bible teacher—this time maybe a bit more provocative, deliberately so. Dale Moody loves to duel verbally so long as he can choose the weapon. And who can equal him in quoting texts and citing contexts and bringing out the main thrust of a passage? Among the Moodyania at Southern Seminary is the story of a student who challenged the position Moody took on a certain

issue. With some confidence in his own position he rattled off a couple of
texts. Moody waited patiently. When the student finished, he buried his ques-
tioner under an avalanche of quotations. The student spluttered, "That's unfair." "What's unfair about it?" Moody wanted to know. "I was just quoting
scriptures." "I know," replied his challenger. "But you do it with such ve-
hemence!"

Scan the Moody bibliography, and you will find little not addressed directly to the Bible or saturated with the Bible. Moody has written commentaries on Ephesians, Romans and the Johannine epistles plus dozens of articles
interpreting portions of the Bible;[1] and many briefer articles for denominational publications. In addition, he has spent years working out a new chronology for the New Testament.[2] The vast majority of other writings would
fall into the category of biblical theology: *The Hope of Glory,* biblical eschatology;[3]*Spirit of the Living God: The Biblical Concepts Interpreted in Context,* biblical pneumatology;[4]*The Word of Truth: A Summary of Christian
Doctrine Based on Biblical Revelation,* a systematizing of what Moody would
call "Bible doctrines" rather than a systematic theology;[5] and major articles
on such issues as the virgin birth or miraculous conception,[6] the church,[7] baptism,[8] the Lord's Supper,[9] the ministry,[10] and the Holy Spirit.[11] Although a
little conversation will disclose that Dale Moody knows his chosen field of

---

[1]*Christ and the Church: An Exposition of Ephesians with Special Application to Some
Present Issues* (Grand Rapids MI: William B. Eerdmans Publishing Co., 1963); "Romans"
in *The Broadman Bible Commentary,* ed. Clifton J. Allen (Nashville: Broadman Press, 1970),
10: 153-286; *The Letters of John* (Waco TX: Word Books, 1970); "God's Only Son: The
Translation of John 3:16 in the Revised Standard Version," *JBL* 72 (1953) 213-19; "Isaiah
7:14 in the Revised Standard Version," *Rev Exp* 50 (1953), 61-68; "The First Epistle of Paul
to the Corinthians (A.D. 55)," ibid., 57 (1960): 450-53.

[2]See "A New Chronology for the New Testament," *Rev Exp* 78 (1981): 211-31.

[3]Grand Rapids MI: William B. Eerdmans Publishing Co., 1964.

[4]Philadelphia: Westminster Press, 1968: Nashville TN: Broadman Press, 1976.

[5]Grand Rapids MI: William B. Eerdmans Publishing Co., 1968.

[6]"On the Virgin Birth of Jesus Christ," *Rev Exp* 50 (1953): 453-62; "The Miraculous
Conception (Part I: The Old Testament)," ibid., 51 (1954): 495-507; "The Miraculous Con-
ception (Part II: The New Testament)," ibid., 52 (1955): 44-54; "The Miraculous Conception
(Part III: The Church Fathers)," ibid., 52 (1955): 310-24; "Virgin Birth," *IDB* 2: 789-91.

[7]"The Nature of the Church," *Rev Exp* 51 (1954): 204-16; "The Nature of the Church,"
in *What is the Church?* ed. Duke K. McCall (Nashville: Broadman Press, 1958) 15-27.

[8]"The Origin of Infant Baptism," in *The Teacher's Yoke,* ed. E. Jerry Vardaman and
James Leo Garrett, Jr. (Waco TX: Baylor University Press, 1964) 189-202.

[9]"The New Testament Significance of the Lord's Supper," in *What Is The Church?,* 79-
96.

[10]"The Ministry of the New Testament," *Rev Exp* 56 (1950): 31-42; "Charismatic and
Official Ministries: A Study of the New Testament Concept," *Int* 19 (1965): 168-81.

[11]"The Holy Spirit and Missions: Visions and Dynamic," *Rev Ed,* 62 (1965): 75-81.

systematic theology as well as any contemporary theologian, he has written as a systematic theologian chiefly in two doctoral dissertations—one at Southern Seminary on "The Problem of Revelation and Reason in the Writings of Emil Brunner" (1947), the other at Oxford University published under the title *Baptism: Foundation for Christian Unity*[12]—and a few major articles.[13] In every one of these, however, Moody has used a single measuring rod: does this square with the Bible? In his Faculty Address delivered at Southern Seminary in 1948, for instance, he faulted American theologians for being "more at home in some philosophical system than in the historical study of the Bible." He proceeded to state unequivocally the supposition on which he would himself do theology. "Upon the solid foundation of historical revelation the structure of sound theology stands."[14] Reviewing "Present (1950) Theological Trends" in Roman Catholic Theology, Dispensationalism, Lundensian theology, and Barthian theology, he found good in each but also criticized each under the searchlight of biblical theology. Roman Catholic theologians depended too heavily on natural theology and too little on the Bible. Dispensationalists negated their conservatism by inappropriate interpretation. Lundensians lacked adequate eschatology. Barth drew too much from Calvin and not enough from the Bible.[15] Insofar as I can discover, Moody has never wavered from the stance he took early on. It is ironic but not really surprising that a person so committed to the biblical revelation should end up under fire from Fundamentalists. For although Dale Moody has planted his feet firmly on the authority of the biblical revelation, he has also accepted modern historical-critical methodology in study of the Bible, and it is precisely this which fundamentalism will not tolerate. "Adjustment of biblical faith to modern science is not as catastrophic as many imagine," he wrote in 1967. "The most catastrophic thing for fundamentalism, still very much alive, is to adjust to the historical study of scripture."[16]

A COMING AND A CALLING

Dale Moody had to *learn* historical criticism; he *inherited* love for the Bible. Born 27 January 1915 on California Creek, south of Stamford, in Jones County, Texas, he grew up in a devout Baptist family. Both his mother, Mat-

---

[12]Philadelphia: Westminster Press, 1967.

[13]"An Introduction to Emil Brunner," *Rev Exp* 44 (1947): 312-30; "The Crux of Christian Theology," ibid., 46 (1949): 164-80; Moody's Faculty Address, "Present Theological Trends (A Review Article)," ibid., 47 (1950): 3-20; "Tabletalk on Theology Tomorrow," ibid., 64 (1967): 341-56; and "The Shaping of Southern Baptist Polity," *Baptist History and Heritage* 14 (July 1979): 2-11.

[14]"The Crux of Christian Theology," *Rev Exp* 46 (1949): 167.

[15]*Rev Exp* 47 (1950): 3-20.

[16]"Tabletalk on Theology Tomorrow," *Rev Exp* 64 (1967): 345.

tie Fuller Moody, and his father, Claud S. Moody, had strong Baptist roots. Dale, however, cites a stream of influence flowing from his great grandfather, John Simmons, one of the key figures in the founding of the Lonesome Dove Baptist Church. His paternal grandmother often admonished him by having him look at this great grandfather's picture and exhorting, ''You look just like your great grandfather. Now you've got to grow up and be a good man just like him. . . . Why, your great grandfather was so devout he wouldn't whip his children on Sunday!''[17] The Moody household included four other children—James Austin, Marie, Lucille, and Virginia.

Dale grew up at Grapevine, now the site of the Dallas-Fort Worth International Airport. At the time, his parents belonged to the church at Lonesome Dove, where his father had lived early in his life. Lonesome Dove was formally known as the United Baptist Church of Jesus Christ, indicative of the merger of Regular and Separate Baptists. The Separate Baptist influence stood out with its emphasis on the homecoming, known as the ''big meeting,'' which drew people from far and near. This church had had a single pastor for forty years.

That pastor, Bill Day, influenced Dale Moody immensely. Moody describes him as ''the most unforgettable preacher I ever knew.'' Day, a self-educated preacher, had ''uncanny'' preaching ability. He took a chapter out of the Bible and simply expounded it in the very way Moody himself has done much of his life. Day had neither college nor seminary training, but he did have real gifts in expository preaching. He did not consult commentaries or other aids. By simply reading the text, he produced solid common sense interpretations. Moody insists that ''Nobody shaped my preaching like Day. It was plain old Bible preaching. He was a Bible preacher. That's what people called him.''[18] In one respect, however, Dale Moody could not follow in Day's footsteps. Day pulled the Lonesome Dove Baptist Church out of the local association and led it to affiliate with the Baptist Missionary Association founded by Ben Bogard.

Conversion and a call to preach came in close succession for Dale Moody. his conversion account has a Pauline ring to it:

> In the summer of 1927, as I was riding my horse through the woods just beyond what is now Grapevine Dam, I made a commitment to Jesus Christ in a little grove that I still visit. This very private and personal experience led me to profess my faith in an evangelistic service at the Grapevine Baptist Church, where I was baptized before the end of the summer.[19]

---

[17]Personal Interview.

[18]Personal Interview.

[19]Dale Moody and Clifton D. Harrison, ''A Texas Tumbleweed,'' Unpublished Paper, 11.

Baptized at Grapevine, Moody transferred his membership to Coppell when his family moved theirs. It was at Coppell that he experienced a call to preach.

This call came after a month of attending revival services under the Tabernacle used by both Baptists and Methodists at Coppell. His mother's family had attended this gathering for years. "After much prayer," Moody related, "a vision of myself in a pulpit preaching convinced me that God was calling me to be a preacher."[20] The next year he tried his gifts and gave a convincing enough display that Coppell Baptist Church first licensed him and then, after the resignation of Lawrence Walker, invited him to be their pastor while he was in his senior year in high school.

CONFIRMING OF A CALLING

Dale moody, like his mentor Bill Day, possesses a wealth of gifts for doing what he has spent his life doing—preaching and teaching the Bible. A photographic memory enabled him to memorize great blocks of scripture—all of the New Testament, parts of it in different versions, and much of the Old Testament. A natural zeal and competitiveness have made him an outstanding student all of his life. His brother James taught him to read before he began the first grade. Two school teachers, Sally Brooks at Coppell Elementary School and Ruth Paddock (later Mrs. Cornell Goerner) at Carrollton High School, sensed his drive and assigned him extra work to "keep him out of mischief." Dale graduated from Carrollton as valedictorian and Best-All-Round Student. He attended Baylor University on both ministerial and athletic scholarships from 1933 to 1936 but dropped out before graduating to study at Dallas Theological Seminary. At Baylor, Henry Trantham equipped him with skills in translating Greek. Here, too, he ranked at the top of most of his classes, but "some other unusual experiences" which he construed as "the filling of the Holy Spirit" triggered an early exit. He returned in 1940 to complete his degree, graduating *cum laude* in 1941.

As a high school student, Moody became involved in a program called The Radio Revival conducted by W. E. Hawkins. On Saturdays Moody did a program for children and thought he might join Hawkins permanently. Not wanting to attend a "post-millenial" school, he declined to go to Southwestern Seminary and instead enrolled at Dallas Theological Seminary. Dallas Theological Seminary's reputation for dispensationalism drew Moody, but in the long run it failed to satisfy his spiritual and vocational needs and his need for freedom. "Much there I liked," he has said, "but I needed more freedom to make my own decisions and form my own beliefs than was cus-

---

[20]Ibid.

tomary there.''[21] Dispensationalists couldn't tolerate Moody's association with
an Assemblies of God preacher named Albert Ott. They wanted to know what
he was doing with those ''Holy Rollers.'' The fact is, a year at Dallas served
chiefly to set the stage for a life-long tryst with dispensationalism, for which
Dallas is the American hub. In a review of ''Present Theological Trends'' in
1950[22], Moody did a careful critique of the dispensationalism of L. S. Chafer,
founder of Dallas Theological Seminary. Years later, he picked apart Hal
Lindsey's eschatology. ''Where the academic and apocalyptic 'theology of
hope' has slain its thousands,'' he wrote, ''the fundamentalist Dispensationalism of Hal Lindsey has slain its ten thousands.''[23] He predicted that ''those
who live until 1988 will find Lindsey a false prophet.''[24] He also wrote a series on millenialism for Baptist state papers distinguishing pre-millenialism
from dispensationalism.[25] Similarly, he criticized vigorously the immensely
popular *Living Bible* for imposing a dispensationalist scheme on the scriptures. ''Not even a person who calls himself a 'strict conservative' has the
right to rewrite the Bible,'' he insisted.[26]

In the summer of 1937 Dale Moody left Dallas and proceeded to Louisville to enroll at The Southern Baptist Theological Seminary. Here he found
a very different atmosphere. In glaring contrast to the ''strait-laced'' and narrow approach of Dallas Theological Seminary Southern offered Moody a
shocking breath of freedom. Of all professors at Southern Moody likes most
to depict himself in the shadow of W. O. Carver. Carver introduced him to
a new world in a course on ''Christianity and Current Thought'' in which the
required text was W. H. Horton's *Contemporary English Theology*, featur-
ing such notables as William Temple and John Oman. Temple's *Nature, Man,
and God* proved to Moody he needed to learn more than the Bible if he would
be a true teacher of the Bible. He would need philosophy and a lot of other
things.

Southern Seminary was the perfect place for someone so intensely interested in teaching and preaching the Bible. From the very beginning, the Seminary had emphasized Bible study, requiring Greek and Hebrew throughout
the entire course of study of those who wished to obtain degrees. The early

---

[21]Ibid.

[22]*Rev Exp* 47 (1950): 3-20.

[23]''The Eschatology of Hal Lindsey,'' *Rev Exp* 72 (1975): 271.

[24]Ibid., 276.

[25]''The Thousand-Year Reign of Christ on the Earth,'' *Word and Way,* 13 January 1977,
4; ''Amillenialism,'' ibid., 20 January 1977, 3; ''Postmillenialism,'' ibid., 27 January 1977,
6; and ''Dispensationalism,'' ibid., 3 February 1977, 5.

[26]''Is the 'Living Bible' Reliable?'' *Baptist Program,* August 1976, 7.

faculty, including W. O. Carver, had all majored in Bible. Complementing that, however, was a breadth of learning and culture which would equip ''the man of God'' rightly to divide the Word of truth (2 Timothy 2:15), the Seminary's motto, engraved on the portico of Norton Hall. As an undergraduate, Moody served as pastor at Highland Park; as a graduate student, at Valley View.

Although Moody completed the full three year course of study at the top of every class, he could not receive his Th.M. degree until he obtained his B.A. from Baylor in 1941. From Baylor he soon returned to the Beeches to pursue a Th.D. under the direction of W. O. Carver. Distinguished work at the graduate level led to his election as a Kent Fellow by the National Council on Religion in Higher Education in 1944. He chose to spend the year studying at Union Theological Seminary and Columbia University in New York City. At Union he served as a Teaching Fellow for Paul Tillich. The year in New York gave him an opportunity to catch up on the philosophy for which Carver had whetted his appetite. He read Plato, Aristotle, Augustine, Thomas Aquinas, Descartes, Spinoza, Leibnitz, and Hegel with characteristic thoroughness. At Union and Columbia Richard Korner ''split his head open'' with great ideas.[27] Many of the works he went through three times as a tutor for students in a course on the history of western thought taught by Henry P. Van Dusen.

In the spring of 1945 the Faculty of The Southern Baptist Theological Seminary invited Moody to return and teach historical theology and the philosophy of religion while he completed his dissertation on ''The Problem of Revelation and Reason in the Writings of Emil Brunner.'' Although he had excellent preparation to discharge this assignment, these subjects stood more on the periphery than in the center of Dale Moody's vocation. The way to the center opened three years later when Harold Tribble, Joseph Emerson Brown Professor of Christian Theology, resigned to assume the presidency of Andover-Newton Theological Seminary. ''When President Ellis A. Fuller asked me to become a permanent professor and teach biblical theology,'' says Moody, ''my heart leaped for joy.''[28]

Never completely satisfied with his preparation, Moody spent the summer of 1948 in Switzerland, thanks to the generosity of President Fuller. He lived in Zurich with Emil Brunner and commuted to Basel to study also with Karl Barth, then the towering theologian of the West. His indebtedness to these two notwithstanding, however, he gained more through contacts with two outstanding biblical theologians also teaching in Basel—Walther Eichrodt and Oscar Cullmann. Eichrodt's famous *Theologie des Alten Testaments* ap-

---

[27]Personal Interview.

[28]''Texas Tumbleweed,'' 12.

peared serially between 1933 and 1939, Cullman's seminal work *Christ and Time* in 1946. The cordial reception both accorded this zealous young teacher struck a deep chord, and Moody has correctly sized up the importance of his meeting with them. "Eichrodt and Cullmann have perhaps been more influential on my theology than Brunner and Barth," he judged. "My preference for biblical theology was by now firmly established."[29] Eichrodt and Cullmann proved immensely useful in the next few years. In teaching biblical theology Moody translated Eichrodt's three volume Old Testament theology, not published in English until 1961, and circulated it in mimeographed form to students. Cullmann's "salvation history" pervaded his entire approach.

CHASING A CALLING

Dale Moody began his career as a professor teaching biblical theology and Christian apologetics, but, as the student body grew during the post-war era and other colleagues joined the Department of Christian Theology, he shifted increasingly in the direction of biblical theology taught under the rubric of systematic theology. He has himself characterized the first ten years of his career, 1948-1957, as "a golden age." It was unquestionably the most creative period in his classroom teaching. By 1957 he had carved his niche in the curriculum and changed it little thereafter. The pattern of courses gives evidence of his preference for biblical theology. From 1949 until 1953 he taught, in addition to systematic theology, theology of the Old Testament and theology of the New Testament, including graduate seminars, and the doctrine of the Holy Spirit. When Wayne E. Ward joined Moody in the Department of Theology in 1952, Moody relinquished Old Testament theology to him. The next year, when Eric Rust, coming from Rawdon College in England, was added to the Faculty, Ward turned over the teaching of Old Testament theology to the latter and began to teach New Testament theology. Meantime, Moody laid out the basic pattern for his own teaching of Bible doctrine. To his course in the doctrine of the Holy Spirit he added undergraduate classes in the Christian doctrine of man, the doctrine of the atonement, and Christian eschatology and graduate seminars in the doctrine of the Trinity, the doctrine of the image of God in man, the doctrine of the virgin birth, and immortality.

Moody's concern for biblical theology stands out not only in the pattern of classes and in his method of doing theology but in his choice of colleagues. Wayne Ward followed his mentor in focusing on biblical theology—first Old and then New Testament. Eric Rust, who gave the Norton lectures at South-

---

[29]Ibid.

ern Seminary in 1953, had already established a reputation in this field with the publication of *Nature and Man in Biblical Thought* and belonged to the same "salvation history" tradition as Moody himself did. Both show the mark of William Temple and Oscar Cullmann.[30] Rust subsequently shifted his teaching increasingly in the direction of Christian apologetics, but he never tossed aside his anchor in biblical theology.

Dale Moody missed the conflict between President Duke K. McCall and members of the Faculty of the School of Theology during the academic year 1957-1958 due to his first sabbatical year spent in Heidelberg.[31] Studying on a Faculty Fellowship, the first of two he received from the American Association of Theological Schools, he spent his time composing articles for the *Interpreter's Dictionary of the Bible*.[32]

A far more significant study leave opened three years later, inaugurating an era of publication. Thanks to the generosity of Newton Rayzor, a Trustee of Southern Seminary, and Mrs. Rayzor, he began a two year stint as a Fellow of Regent's Park College at Oxford University in 1961. There he wrote his first books—*Christ and the Church* (1963) and *The Hope of Glory* (1964)—and did research for the Doctor of Philosophy, completed in 1966. This degree opened new vistas for Moody. When his dissertation appeared under the title *Baptism: Foundation for Christian Unity,* he received an invitation to lecture at the Gregorian University in Rome, the second Protestant and the first Baptist ever to teach there, in 1969-1970. He also had numerous invitations to teach in other schools, but his strong commitment to Southern Seminary held him fast. Meantime he was invited to become a member of the Faith and Order Commission of The World Council of Churches. In 1973 and 1976 he was invited to participate in The Ecumenical Institute for Advanced Theological Research (Tantur) in Jerusalem. In 1973 he began the writing of his systematic theology, completed in 1977 but not published until 1981.[33] In 1976 he initiated research for "A New Chronology for the Life and Letters of Paul."

No other faculty member at Southern Seminary has been as open to or received as wide ecumenical notice as Dale Moody. His ecumenical spirit and outlook extend deep into his past. At Coppell he participated in ecumenical

---

[30]See my article on "Eric Charles Rust: Apostle to an Age of Science and Technology," in *Science, Faith and Revelation: An Approach to Christian Philosophy,* ed. Robert E. Patterson (Nashville: Broadman Press, 1979) 13-25.

[31]On this incident see my article on "Southern Baptist Theological Seminary," *Encyclopedia of Southern Baptists* (Nashville: Broadman Press, 1971), 1978-83.

[32]"Only Begotten," *IDB* 3: 604; "Shekinah," ibid., 4:317-19; "Stumbling Block," ibid., 449; "Virgin Birth," ibid., 789-91.

[33]*The Word of Truth: A Summary of Christian Doctrine Based on Biblical Revelation* (Grand Rapids MI: William B. Eerdmans Publishing Co., 1981.)

meetings. At Waco, while a student at Baylor, and at Dallas, while a student at Dallas Theological Seminary, he preached in the Assemblies of God church, developing an intimate friendship with the pastor of Bethlehem Temple, Albert Ott, despite Baptist disdain for Pentecostals. His mentor W. O. Carver, President Ellis A. Fuller, and other professors at Southern Seminary broadened his ecumenical horizons still more. Nevertheless, Moody blazed a trail of his own all over the Christian world. In Louisville he has participated in an ecumenical fellowship composed of Protestant ministers, Roman Catholic priests, and Jewish rabbis. He often preaches in other churches or ecumenical groups. His international involvement, therefore, should not have surprised anyone.

CLOUDING A CALLING

Moody had an illustrious career as a teacher and theologian. One of the most popular Bible preachers and teachers in the Southern Baptist Convention, he has spoken at all level of denominational life—local churches, associational meetings, state conventions, and the Southern Baptist Convention. He has addressed writings not only to scholars but also to people in the pew, students on the campuses, and persons outside the religious sphere. At Southern Seminary he enjoyed almost unequalled popularity with students, regularly attracting large classes and enthusiastic response.

Like all persons who have something significant to say, however, he did not escape controversy and criticism. The fact is, Moody has operated with the style of the old frontier controversialists or the ancient Latin Church Father Tertullian of Carthage who aimed to get attention and usually succeeded. Few students who matriculated at Southern Seminary during the Moody years will forget klatches in the student center or hallways with Dale Moody at the center making rapier-like points and then deliberately inciting a response.

One issue, however, clouded the final years of this brilliant teacher/ preacher, the issue of apostasy. Had this matter not had solid biblical bases, of course, it would not have taken hold of Moody the way it did. Given his absolute commitment to the authority of the Bible, however, he saw no option. Ironically those whose high view of the Scriptures Moody would approximate became the persons most alarmed by his views on apostasy.

From the beginning of his career Moody had a special concern about the effect of the popular cliche "Once saved, always saved" circulating among Southern Baptists. In 1941, while completing his final year at Baylor, he attracted public notice as pastor of Calvary Baptist Church in Mexia, Texas with two sermons he preached on the question of apostasy. He had formed his views through study of the Greek New Testament and Robertson's *Word Pictures in the New Testament.*[34] "Any profession of faith that does not produce fruit does not have a claim to eternal security or genuine salvation," he said at the opening of an article on "Eternal Security" for the *Baptist Adult Union Quarterly* in 1955.[35] He based his argument on the parable of the soils (Luke 8:4-15) and Paul's "song of God's sovereign love" in Romans 8:31-39. Year by year students heard Moody marshal powerful scriptural arguments on the same point.

Moody's long standing concern for authentic faith took a wry turn in 1961 as a result of lectures given on "The Christology of Colossians" at Oklahoma Baptist University in Shawnee, June 27-30. Subsequent to these lectures, the Oklahoma County Association passed a resolution attacking Moody for "deviations" from "Baptist teaching" on four points: apostasy or falling from grace, receiving persons baptized in other denominations without rebaptism, practicing open communion, and affirming the ecumenical movement.[36] Moody fired quick replies to each of the charges to Sam W. Scantlan and to the association,[37] citing his agreement with views held by predecessors, on the question of apostasy, in particular A. T. Robertson. Unfortunately these may have fueled the flames rather than doused them. Moody's long time friend Chauncey Daley, then Editor of *Western Recorder,* put his finger on the pulse of the problem in a defense of his former professor:

> Moody has two virtues that sometimes work against him and the acceptance of his views. One, he says what he says with overpowering force. This produces enthusiastic acceptance by those who agree with him but elicits resentment from those who disagree with him. This apparently happened in Oklahoma.
>
> Two, he takes the New Testament so seriously as to be unmindful of traditional Baptist beliefs. To take the New Testament seriously is always dangerous especially if you think it contradicts traditional theology. At least Moody is honest and doesn't gloss over New Testament passages which are hard to make compatible with certain traditional Baptist positions.[38]

---

[34]*The Mexia Daily News,* 18 August 1941, reported that Moody refuted both "once saved, always saved," and the possibility of repeated restorations. His own view was: "The Bible teaches that saved people can so sin as to be lost. Again the Bible teaches that such a person is an apostate and cannot be restored to fellowship with God." He cited numerous scriptures. Article quoted in full by Clark Richard Youngblood, "The Question of Apostasy in Southern Baptist Thought since 1900: A Critical Evaluation" (Ph.D. diss., Southern Baptist Theological Seminary, 1978) 152.

[35]"What We Believe About Eternal Security," *Baptist Adult Union Quarterly,* 18 December 1955, 36.

[36]*Western Recorder,* 10 August 1961, 5.

[37]"Dale Moody's Reply to Resolution Adopted in Oklahoma City," *Baptist Press,* 4 August 1961, 4-7.

[38]Editorial, *Western Recorder,* 24 August 1961, 4-5.

From an administrative standpoint danger lurked not in Moody's handling of the Scriptures but in the direct challenge he posed to Article XIII of the *Abstract of Principles,* the Seminary's official doctrinal standard which all Faculty members must agree to "teach in accordance with and not contrary to." According to Moody's personal recollection, when he joined the Faculty in 1948, he explained to President Ellis A. Fuller the reservations he had concerning the way in which this article conflicted directly with Scripture. These notwithstanding, Fuller recommended him to the Trustees, Moody insisted, "with the full knowledge of my beliefs and with full knowledge that I agreed with Robertson on Hebrews 6:4-6. . . . "[39] During the controversy in 1961, Moody defended his signing of the *Abstract* on the grounds that he had been faithful to Scripture and to the teachings of such Southern Seminary luminaries as John A. Broadus, A. T. Robertson, and W. O. Carver. He attributed the problem of the *Abstract* to a scribal error first made by the Elder William Collins of Petty France Church in London when he revised the Westminster Confession of Faith in preparing the Second London Confession in 1677. When the *Abstract of Principles* was adopted in 1858, it remained uncorrected. The Elder Collins substituted "they will be renewed again unto repentance" for "it is impossible to renew them again unto repentance" of Hebrews 6:6. Moody proceeded to explain that he was "unable to endorse an error that contradicts the Scriptures that I accept as supreme in all matters of faith and order."[40] The Trustees of the Seminary chose at this time to take no action against Moody. Fortunately the controversy had a chance to die down somewhat as a result of Moody's departure for Oxford for a two-year stay. The attention of his attackers, in the meantime, shifted to Ralph Elliott, Professor of Old Testament at Midwestern Baptist Theological Seminary in Kansas City, Missouri, with the appearance of Elliott's *The Message of Genesis*.

Matters did not turn out so well when the controversy surfaced again after the publication of *The Word of Truth* in 1981. From 1961 on, Duke K. McCall, President of Southern Seminary, had been very circumspect about Moody's reservations concerning Article XIII of the *Abstract of Principles*. Although he zealously guarded freedom of the classroom during his presidency, McCall used the occasion of Moody's retirement in 1980 at age sixty-five to require him to clarify his views concerning the *Abstract of Principles* and to sign the document again. Moody signed, but he attached an edited copy of the *Abstract* expressing his reservations about Article XIII's conflict with Scripture.

----

[39]Draft of letter of explanation and defense addressed but not sent to Penrose St. Amant, Dean of the School of Theology, Southern Seminary, dated 3 January 1962, 4; cited by Youngblood, "The Question of Apostasy," 155.

[40]Revised letter of explanation and defense to St. Amant, dated 3 January 1962, 1-2; cited by Youngblood, ibid., 159.

When *The Word of Truth* rolled off the presses in 1981, it received favorable responses even among conservative evangelicals. As anticipated, however, the section on apostasy evoked angry reactions from some. The Little Red River Baptist Association in Arkansas directed a letter to President McCall asking how long the Seminary would continue to employ Moody.[41] As debate waxed hot in Arkansas, the editor of the *Arkansas Baptist Newsmagazine,* Everett Sneed, requested Moody's reply. Moody responded by sending the section of *The Word of Truth* dealing with apostasy. Moody was then asked to address the annual pre-convention Pastors' Conference on the subject on 15 November 1982. Never one to back away from debate, Moody accepted the invitation.

Trying to avert a crisis, Roy Honeycutt, newly elected president of Southern Seminary, discussed the issue with Moody and recommended that he decline to speak. Moody left Louisville for a week. While he was gone, Honeycutt sent him a letter dated 1 November, indicating that, since Moody had made it clear he could not teach "in accordance with and not contrary to" the *Abstract of Principles,* it was his duty as President to ask Moody either to retire or resign, or he would have to consider other alternatives. When Moody received this letter upon his return to Louisville 8 November, he interpreted the last point to mean "or be fired." He wavered somewhat regarding the invitation to address the Pastors' Conference, first declining on 11 November and then deciding to go ahead on 13 November.

Moody's candid and spirited defense of his views, based on Hebrews 10:26 and 2 Peter 2:20 as "the clearest of the 48 passages in the New Testament" warning against apostasy, drew polite attention and applause, but it also evoked barbs and bitterness. Messengers to the Convention passed a resolution on 17 November calling for the Trustees of Southern Seminary to "consider the termination" of Professor Moody. Curiously they based their objection on the 1963 *Baptist Faith and Message's* statement that "all true believers endure to the end, and are kept by the power of God through faith unto salvation," an article Moody himself had helped to draft and with which he agrees. They did not charge violation of the *Abstract of Principles,* which, from the Seminary trustees' viewpoint, would have been far more serious.[42]

The controversy grew more and more contorted despite efforts both within and outside the Seminary to bring it under control. Moody himself admitted he subscribed to ninety-eight percent or more of the *Abstract,* but he counted his point about Article XIII a matter of integrity and faithfulness to Scripture.

---

[41]Personal letter to Dr. McCall, 11 December 1981.

[42]"Messengers Ask for Dismissal of Southern Seminary Professor," *Arkansas Baptist Newsmagazine,* 25 November 1982, 6-7.

Faced with an already volatile denominational situation created by contro-
·versy over biblical inerrancy, the Trustees of the Seminary voted to cut short
Moody's teaching beyond the date of his retirement by two years. Moody had
already taught two years as Senior Professor (1980-1982) and been elected
Professor of Christian Theology without tenure in 1982. Since this contract
bore no date of termination, the Board of Trustees set the date of termination
for 31 July 1984 to coincide with the end of a leave of absence Moody was
scheduled to take in 1983-1984 to teach in Hong Kong by invitation of the
Foreign Mission Board[43] of the Southern Baptist Convention. President Honeycutt, judging it ''not in the best interest of the Seminary to offer Professor
Moody a fourth teaching contract for the period of 1984-85,'' set the date for
the termination of Moody's teaching responsibilities at the Seminary on 10
June 1983.[44]

The sad outcome of this affair confirms the portrait of Dale Moody which
I have attempted to paint in this article. Moody has staked his life on the conviction that the Scriptures are the word of truth; to this truth we must subor-
dinate everything else. Doubtless we will find inconsistencies in Moody's life,
but on this matter he has acted with such terrible consistency as to beget tragedy. His response to the shortening of his teaching career was:

> I insist on revising the *Abstract* until it is in line with the Scriptures and the
> *Statement [of the Baptist Faith and Message]* of 1963. . . . I believe with
> no reservations that the *Abstract* is to be judged by the Scriptures as Article
> I and XVIII of the *Abstract* say. This is the real issue that has determined
> my termination of teaching one year early, but I have only begun to fight
> for the supreme authority of Scripture and for liberty of conscience under
> the authority of Scripture. If the *Statement of the Baptist Faith and Message*
> [of 1925] can be revised, why is the *Abstract of Principles*, with errors
> reaching back to 1677, considered beyond revision?[45]

Here we must ask whether the real tragedy lies with Moody or with the
Seminary and the Convention. The answer to Moody's quite legitimate question is: if the Board of Trustees begin to revise the *Abstract*, they will open
the way to a radical revision almost certainly including Article I, on which
Moody himself places so much emphasis. Fundamentalists would be quick
to impose an inerrantist statement that would constrict use of the historical-
·critical method in interpreting Scripture. When the founding fathers drafted
the *Abstract* in 1858, they made one highly significant adjustment in the
statement they drew from the Second London Confession of 1677: they sub-

---

[43]Report of the Trustees, *Western Recorder,* 27 April 1983: 3, 9.

[44]President's Statement, ibid., 9.

[45]*Western Recorder,* 27 April 1983, 9.

stituted ''authoritative'' for ''infallible.'' Scriptures, according to the *Abstract,* ''are the only sufficient, certain and *authoritative* rule of all saving knowledge, faith and *obedience.*'' One does not have to reflect long to realize how far this statement stands from the one Fundamentalists would impose, declaring that Scriptures are inerrant scientifically, historically, philosophically, and theologically.

A CALLING FULFILLED

The cloud that cast a shadow over the late years of Dale Moody's career must not be seen out of proportion; it is small and inconsequential when viewed across the broad horizon where the sun has shone brightly. W. A. Criswell, Pastor of the First Baptist Church of Dallas, called Moody's *The Word of Truth* ''one of the finest volumes in present theological literature'' and complimented Moody himself as ''truly and verily a learned man of God, . . . as learned as Karl Barth.''[46] Moody has obviously not written as voluminously as Barth, but the remark rings true. Dale Moody represents the very best piety that persistent, painstaking, prayerful, and probing attention to the Bible can produce. If Southern Baptists have had a world-class Bible teacher and preacher, it has been Moody. At times he may have been loud and contentious and overly provocative in his desire to bring the Word that pierces hearts and minds; yet even those whom his views disturbed most will bear witness to the power with which he has delivered the Word.

When *The Word of Truth* appeared, I noticed that Moody was not carrying his Greek New Testament around as his custom had been but instead a copy of his book. When chidingly I called this to his attention, he replied, ''But it's all in here!'' If anyone has put the whole of The Scriptures, especially the New Testament, in one book, it would be Dale Moody. Yet I doubt whether even he has succeeded at that. I think, rather, that it is all in Dale Moody himself. It is his heart and mind and soul and strength.

---

[46]W. A. Criswell, personal letter, 8 March 1982.

REVELATION
AND THE BIBLE

BOB E. PATTERSON
BAYLOR UNIVERSITY
WACO TX 79998

Revelation is the idea that what has previously been hidden is now made plain, or that the undisclosed is now revealed. In a theistic context it suggests that the unknown divine becomes a known God with a personal name. In a Christian framework, revelation has ordinarily been divided into two categories, for ease of discussion.

GENERAL REVELATION

General revelation is the notion that I, on my own initiative, can discover something about both the existence and character of God through nature, history, and my own conscience, reason, and will. If God exists, I need to know it. I cannot be assured that God is friendly toward me until I am convinced that He "is"; so my pursuit of religious knowledge is not a trivial matter. Religion cannot thrive on ignorance.

I know a variety of things with some certainty. I know bodies. I know other minds, and that is probably easier than knowing bodies. For example, we know much of the mind of Christ through the four Gospels, but we do not know what his body looked like. I know my own mind, and I know my own thoughts apart from the senses of my body. Again, I know values and universals. For example, I am aware of truth and beauty although I cannot measure them as I would my own body. Further, I know God as a Mind. He does not have a body as I do, but I relate to Him as consciousness to consciousness.

What evidence is there in general revelation for the astounding claim that "I know God"? To observe intelligently is a rare gift, and disciplined insight a precious commodity. Since some evidence is better than other evidence, we need to look for converging lines of evidence and as many lines as possible. Even good evidence may not dispel theoretical doubt, but security can lie in the phenomenon of cumulative, convergent evidence.

Elton Trueblood, the Quaker philosopher, once told me how he came to the concept of cumulative, positive evidence. When he was a student in Chicago, a child was kidnapped and held for ransom. Her abductor was arrested and brought to trial. There were four lines of evidence brought against the accused man in court, but no one line alone was enough to convict him. First, he was found with the child, but he said that he had come upon the child by accident. Second, the ransom money was discovered in his possession, but he said that he found the money at the same time he found the child. Third, the child's nurse identified him as the kidnapper, but since she was under severe strain her sensory impressions were not reliable. Fourth, the accused man finally confessed and said, "I did it." But by then twelve men had come forward before the Chicago news media and said, "I did it," most likely to gain public fame. No one line of evidence was enough to convict the accused, but the jury added the four converging lines and together they said "guilty."

There are converging lines of evidence in general revelation that could lead one to say, "It is more reasonable to believe that the God of Abraham, Isaac, and Jacob 'is' than to believe that He 'is not.'" We can look at several features of the known world for verification. No single feature is conclusive corroboration of the theistic hypothesis, but together their cumulative effect is impressive. We will turn to five different avenues of experience for our evidence—science, morality, aesthetics, history, and religion.[1]

First, we instinctively point to nature because to the average person the cosmos is incomprehensible apart from divine purpose. Evidence from nature is not the weightiest of the five strands of evidence, but we are right to start here. If God the Creator really is, we would expect the natural order to declare his glory and show his handiwork.

Modern science assumes that the world, which existed a long time before we came on the scene, is intelligible to a considerable degree. Science tells us that the world is not self-explanatory, and that nature points beyond itself for an explanation. For example, the Second Law of Thermodynamics hints

---

[1]David Elton Trueblood, *Philosophy of Religion* (New York: Harper & Brothers Publishers, 1957) 79-158. These arguments are taken from Trueblood's analysis.

that the universe could not have originated without a source of energy outside itself and cannot forever sustain itself. Another example is found in the theory of biological evolution which implies that human minds, a product of nature, could only have arisen as the product of Mind. Mind is not an accident of nature, nor is nature alien to mind. Today modern science may strengthen the belief in God.

Our second line of evidence comes from our concern with moral values. Nature may tell us little more than that divine thought is there, but our moral life hints that a Righteous One is behind the cosmos. For the thinking person moral experience would be an absurdity unless there were a Divine One to whom our conscience refers and to whom we are disobedient when we are immoral. We are greatly concerned with what we ought to be or ought to do, and the moral demands are very impressive. There is no way to discuss our lives without discussing our ethical concerns. Our conscience is both permanent and universal.

The moral argument for God's existence follows this pattern: first, moral experience points to an objective moral order beyond ourselves; and second, an objective moral order is meaningful only if there is a Divine Lawgiver (God) to back it up. There is no way for a moral law to exist by itself. I don't invent morality, but I discover it because it is already there ahead of me. Morality has no meaning except to a mind, so there must be a superhuman Mind or God to give significance to moral conduct.

The third line of argument for God's existence comes from the consideration of beauty. Just as there is mind in science and mind in morality, so there is mind in the experience of beauty. The argument runs like this: the painter at the canvas is producing a work of beauty by long disciplined effort and patient thought. His work is not an accident but the expression of his mind. Our hearts leap with joy when we see the beauty in his work, and for a moment our mind matches his mind. Our aesthetic experience always involves a recognition of purpose in the beauty we behold.

When we shift from the canvas to the prodigious beauty of the world we have the same experience. We are driven to the conception of the Divine Artist. If God does exist, natural beauty is what we would expect to find. Just as we do not invent morality, so we do not invent beauty, but we are claimed by it when we see it. Fashion and taste may play a part in our appreciation of beauty, but beauty in nature is an objective reality outside of ourselves. Beauty in the natural order is the self-justifying expression of the Divine Mind.

The fourth line of evidence looks at the total sweep of human history, its wonder, its purpose, and its logic. Here the emphasis is upon the divine guiding hand in the entire saga of human events. The Hebrew people were the first to develop this historical argument for the existence of God. The Exodus from Egypt became to the Old Testament people the central symbol of a sheer miracle of deliverance. As the people of ancient Israel looked back over their experience and its emerging pattern, they felt compelled to ascribe their creation and preservation to God. Christians looked at the triumph of their own faith and drew the same conclusion—''God did it.''

But human history is larger than the Hebrew-Christian traditions, and historical coincidence is not an adequate explanation for the process, direction, and purpose we see in the long sweep of events. The story is a large one and goes back much further than human history. It is only by the most delicate balance that thinking humans could have emerged to recognize the true, the good, and beautiful. The billions of years that it took for life to come from matter on our planet is one continuous story, and it looks as if it were guided by an infinite purpose. The whole process makes sense if it was meant to produce free personalities. This does not prove God's existence, but it is consistent with a belief in divine purpose. Any one event might be the result of chance, but it is too hard to believe that the entire story is an accident.

The fifth strand of evidence comes from religious experience. The first four lines are basically inferential, and at best are grounded in reasonable postulates. But if I can point to a personal experience with God, I not only add a fifth strand to the rope of evidence but add strength to the other strands as well. If I, along with millions of others, report a direct and intimate experience with the Divine, then reflective people may well accept the empirical approach as the major argument for theism.

Elton Trueblood says that thoughtful people will also establish a fourfold test to assure themselves that a reported religious experience is not just a purely private matter. This validating process will be quite similar to that used in sense experience, and is as follows: first, the number of people reporting an experience of God will be examined. The finding is that millions of people of all types in all ages of history have witnessed to such an experience. Second, the character of those reporting such must be guaranteed, since they could be telling a lie. No doubt, some of them have been scoundrels, but many of them have been accounted trustworthy on all other matters and cannot be discounted. Third, their reports must harmonize to a certain degree. And there is a substantial core of agreement: they say that they have had a sense of awe before Another; they tell of a sense of new life which comes from a Divine Source; and, what is given in the encounter is not so much information but the sense of a Presence. Fourth, lives should be changed as a result of such an experience. A careful look will show, for example, that a new happiness has come to the religious, an abiding joy that can live with pain and hardship. When these four tests are met, then religious experience becomes one of the strongest evidences for God's existence.

Yet there are millions of fellow citizens who do not believe in a personal God, and they usually cite one or more of seven reasons for their unbelief.[2] The first and most practical reason given by the atheist is that multitudes of high-minded people have no personal awareness of God. They conclude that those who tell of "encountering God" are deluded. They feel that their own experience of "Godlessness" is normal and regard religious belief at best as purely subjective. This is not so much an argument against God as a sad witness to an "eclipse of God." If it were an argument, it could easily be countered by pointing to one authentic experience of God by someone such as St. Francis of Assisi. The case for atheism is not so strong as it appears, for there are telling rebuttals for each of the seven major bases of unbelief in our century.

The second reason why many moderns reject theistic faith is their judgment that such faith is inconsistent with the scientific method. Several years ago I did a television debate with the atheist Madalyn Murray O'Hair, and she mentioned this charge against belief in God. I reminded her that Sir Isaac Newton, one of the founders of modern science, was a profoundly religious person and actually wrote commentaries on biblical books. Newton felt that religion and the scientific view of reality blended very well. Thirdly, others reject belief in God because they think it produces passivity in the face of social injustice. Mrs. O'Hair, in our debate, raised this objection as well, so I tried to show her that religious people had also been a catalyst for social change. Martin Luther King, Jr., a Baptist pastor, was the prime mover in the civil rights movement of the 1960s. Each of the seven arguments for atheism has an element of truth and should be taken seriously. We should not try to evade them, and we can learn from them.

Atheistic arguments four, five, and six are these: belief in God is untrue because it can be explained as an objectification of purely human wishes and needs; it may be rejected because most statements about God are essentially ambiguous; and, belief in a sovereign God is inconsistent with human freedom.

The seventh and most serious objection to belief in God is also the oldest one—the extent and intensity of human suffering. If many facts cannot be explained *unless* God is, then the evil of unmerited suffering cannot be understood *if* God is. For an atheist the unjust pain suffered by innocent persons would demand no special explanation, but when he tries to believe that the universe is governed by a good and loving God he is faced with difficulties. The problem presents itself to the rational mind in this fashion: if God is good

---

[2]S. Paul Schilling, *God In An Age of Atheism* (Nashville: Abingdon Press, 1969) 115-34. These arguments are taken from Schilling's analysis.

but cannot lower the amount of evil in the world, then he is incompetent; but if God is all powerful and will not put a stop to suffering, then he is unkind and morally inferior to some of his creatures. Thus many moderns cannot combine faith in God with Auschwitz. Further, they have been unsatisfied with the five common arguments that have been seriously proposed as solutions, namely: that suffering is a just punishment for sin; that evil is an illusion; that evil is necessary in the struggle to become better moral people; that God would like to help but cannot; and that we should stoically "grin and bear it" without question.

The humble believer in God takes seriously the stumbling block of evil, but he feels that the reasons for his faith are so great that he can weather even this storm. Like Job, he knows that suffering is too large for his finite mind, but he believes there *is* a solution to the problem of evil though his mind is too ignorant to reach it. The believer knows that when God created us as independent people he also produced a situation in which evil could arise and spread. God's love and sentimental kindness are not the same thing, and our own selfish immorality is the price we pay for our moral freedom. God did not cause our egotism, but he can forgive and overcome it. We cannot be real people unless we have choices, and when we make bad choices we harm ourselves and others. A loving God will always try to persuade us to be good to each other rather than compelling us. Even when we suffer the outrages of cancer or tornadoes, we believe in the final justice of God. The argument runs like this: since God is just, but justice is never perfectly accomplished in this life, there must be a life everlasting in which justice is perfectly accomplished. But this says as much about the character of God as it does about His existence, and the character of God is the subject of special revelation in our next section.

Dale Moody, holding that there is a genuine revelation of God outside the special revelation of Scriptures says, "a general revelation of God is possible in creation at any time, in any place, and to any person."[3] Moody makes the point that the supreme revelation comes in the Son of God, but it is not the sole revelation. In estimating the value of this indirect revelation he says, "Guilt before God is gauged by the light people have, and those who follow the light they have will surely be accepted by God."[4]

SPECIAL REVELATION

If general revelation is the universal knowledge of God available to all of us at all times and all places, special revelation is, on the other hand, God's particular communication of himself to special people who are ready to re-

---

[3]Dale Moody, *The Word of Truth* (Grand Rapids MI: William B. Eerdmans Publishing Co., 1981) 58-59.

[4]Ibid., 62.

ceive him, at special times, and in special ways. This uncovering or manifestation of God is more particularized and detailed than general revelation,
and it is designed to lead us into a personal acquaintance with God. General
revelation is the springboard that takes us into this intimate relationship with
God, but general revelation alone lacks the warm presence of God that we
need.

General revelation is a diffuse, scattered light, whereas special revelation
is a focused beam. In general revelation I may know that God is, but I do not
know his name. When I become aware of my own finitude, the disorders of
existence, and my approaching death, I raise the questions of "Who am I?"
and "What is Being?" But my awareness of Divine Being doesn't mean that
I know God as Father, Son, and Holy Spirit. I may arrive at certain truths
about God on my own (since all truth is God's truth), but to arrive at the point
of a personal introduction to God, I need more help. It is the difference between seeing by starlight and seeing in sunlight, or between an inactive acquaintance with and the building of a personal friendship with God. Because
of my own sin and guilt, my need for special revelation becomes acute. Dale
Moody says, "a doctrine of revelation that includes a general revelation of
God in all creation and in every human conscience, plus the special revelation
of God in the historical events of the Old Testament as promise, with the supreme revelation of God in Jesus Christ, including both his first coming and
the Great Apocalypse of God in the future at his second appearing, is required
for our time."[5]

A redemptive fellowship implies that God's particular style of revelation
of himself is always personal. God, as subject, gives of and from himself to
me, another subject, in a personal covenant. What God reveals is primarily
himself as Divine Person. But since God is transcendent and lies outside our
sensory experience, he must disclose himself in our categories of thought and
language. God uses our ordinary and natural experiences to show himself,
but these ordinary experiences become filled with a unique content. The like-
ness between our language and divine truth means that the words we use for
God's revelation of himself are always analogical.

Whatever angle of approach, root metaphor, or model we choose to express the fact of God's revelation should be submitted to several questions.
Is our model faithful to the Bible? Is it free from internal self-contradiction
and is it plausible? Does it illuminate all our other experiences, and does it
enhance the quality of our moral and intellectual life? Does it help us to understand the religious experience of others and assist us in exchanging insights with them? The model presented below, then, attempts to meet these
criteria.[6]

---

[5]Ibid., 61.

[6]Avery Dulles, S.J., *Models of Revelation* (New York: Doubleday & Company, Inc., 1983)
3-114.

What model, or angle of approach, will serve us best as we speak of God's special revelation of himself? It will be one that emphasizes both the divine deeds as well as the divine speech, a complex of events and words, or the "mighty acts" of God in history, along with his telling us about himself, his plans, and his will. The Bible is a record of numerous historical events in which God has made himself known in a special place (the Holy Land) through a special group of people (the Holy Nation). These deeds of God through historical events are revelations of his nature. First, God reveals himself *in* a series of historical events, and we infer something of the character of God from the way he has acted in the biblical happenings. Second, God reveals himself *through* historical events in such a personal way that he comes into an individual subjective relationship with us. By means of the event we actually meet God himself. Third, God so reveals himself in events that historical happenings actually are revelation. The actions of God are seen *as* history, an objective revelation of a literal character. The major themes of biblical history are God's great deeds.

The other half of this Deed-Word model emphasizes the speech of God as it is mediated through the Old Testament prophets and the New Testament apostles. Since God is spiritual and does not have bodily parts, his words come through human language (by holy men, in a holy book and as an incarnate person). God's speech may take the form of audible words, a silent inner hearing, a dream or vision, created thoughts in the mind, the proper interpretation of an historical event of the past or predictive prophecy about the future, or through the life and words of his unique Son, Jesus Christ. Christ is the most complete form of God's Deed-Word: in Christ we see redemptive history in its most concentrated form; and, the teaching-preaching of Jesus is God himself speaking. In Jesus God's act and God's word come together and we find in him the revelation of the Father. In Jesus we meet the divine personally and we also learn real, objective, rational information about divine things. Revelation is both a person-to-person saving relationship and the learning of truths about God. It is a belief *in* God (trust) and a belief *about* God (assenting knowledge). As God personally meets us he tells us who he is. The words of worship and prayer go hand-in-hand with the language of theological discourse.

There are several advantages to this Deed-Word model for revelation. First, it holds in balance the delicate tension between revelation as history, doctrinal statements, and personal interior experience of communion with God. Second, it guards the utter holiness and transcendence of God by letting God reveal himself at whenever time and to whatever person he so chooses. Third, it points to our responsible faith-acceptance of revelation with its implied notion that revelation shifts our perspective about God and transforms our attitude toward each other. And fourth, it is comprehensive enough to open up dialogue with those who have not moved beyond general revelation, with those Christians who have a different model of revelation, and with those outside the Christian faith who have a different view of the Divine.

This Deed-Word way of seeing revelation implies that the revelation can be written down and preserved in an inspired Bible that may also be termed revelation. The pattern would be something like this: first, God revealed himself in a complex pattern of historical events and words such as the Exodus. God gave himself to Moses in a personal, saving way and at the same time gave new information about himself. Second, he illumined the mind of Moses (inspiration) properly to understand the events taking place in the Nile Valley and to understand correctly the new disclosure of God's nature. Third, Moses accurately conveyed this revelation to the Israelites in his preaching and teaching. Fourth, when Moses and later writers wrote down Moses' oral words, the Bible began to emerge in the believing community in later ages. Fifth, I (in the twentieth century) experience the same revelation that Moses did (or Peter or Paul did) as I hear the words of the Bible. The Holy Spirit so guided MOses, Jeremiah, John, and others that their account of God's revelation has now become the written form of the Word of God through which God encountered me in a saving way. This view of the written word of revelation implies that the Bible writers were using more than their own heightened insights; they were directed by the Holy Spirit to such an extent that we have the exact Bible that God wants us to have. The inspiration came from God, but the Holy Spirit pressed into service all the peculiarities of the writer so that Paul's letters, for example, were uniquely characteristic of Paul. This avoids a dictation model of inspiration while emphasizing the trustworthiness and authority of the Bible. Inspiration, like the original revelation, then, involves both the writer and the writing.

When we say that the Bible is fully inspired, trustworthy, dependable, and is just the book that God wants us to have, we raise the topic of most heated debate among today's conservative Christians—''inerrancy.'' Inerrancy is the doctrine that the Bible is truthful in all of its teachings. The Bible, when its statements are understood in the original cultural setting in which they were expressed and understood in the light of the purpose for which they were written, is inerrant. This definition puts the emphasis equally upon proper interpretation and proper text. But not every conservative Christian would agree with my understanding of inerrancy. Some conservatives hold that the Bible deliberately teaches exact scientific and historical data, and that apparent discrepancies in the Bible can and must be explained away.[7] A closely

---

[7]Millard J. Erickson, *Christian Theology* (Grand Rapids MI: Baker Book House, 1983) 2: 222-24.

allied position says that the Bible is not a purposeful book of science, medi-
cine, history, and so forth, but when it does speak on these topics its asser-
tions are fully true. A third approach says that the Bible may have
contradictions in science, and such, but that is of no consequence since it is
inerrant in its teachings on salvation. (That is, God never intended to reveal
science to the biblical writers.) Fourth, there are conservatives who say that
the Bible inerrantly accomplishes its purpose by bringing us into a personal,
saving relationship with Christ. Lastly, there are conservatives who say that
''inerrancy'' is a distracting way of looking at the Bible for five different reasons: (A) it imposes a precision alien to the biblical writers; (B) it diverts our
attention from the main purpose of the Bible, which is salvation; (C) it en-
courages superficial scholarship over fear that one error may collapse the faith;
(D) it imposes a philosophical category that is alien to the Bible; and (E) it is
defensive, whereas the Bible is confident about itself. The recent inerrancy
debate grew out of a concern to affirm a supernatural revelation of authoritative, cognitive truth, but in the long run it may prove to be a ''false flap''
for conservative Christians, because when inerrancy is carefully defined it
seems to be indistinguishable from the high view of the Bible held by many
non-inerrantists.

Sophisticated, qualified inerrancy hardly differs from traditional views
of the Bible that take it to be God's final written Word. For example, Carl
F. H. Henry, the dean of evangelical theologians, has given us one of the best
statements on inerrancy that most evangelicals can assent to. Negatively,
Henry says that modern technological precision should not be expected of the
biblical writers, nor should we demand of them only non-symbolic language.
Further, we should not demand that New Testament writers quote the Old
Testament with verbal exactitude, nor is personal faith in Christ dispensable
even if we have a perfect book, nor does evangelical orthodoxy follow au-
tomatically from holding to inerrancy. Henry has tried to correct the error of
''over belief'' by his qualifiers of what inerrancy is not. Positively, he says
that inerrancy does imply that scientific matters, for example, are true when
they are part of the express message of the Bible. Again, the very words of
the Bible are true, and not just the thought and concepts of the writers. Further, only the original manuscripts of the Bible writers are error-free, not
modern translations.[8]

Finally, the Deed-Word model of revelation affirms that the Bible is the
final written authority for the believer. The Bible, since it is the expression
of God's will for us, has the right to define what we believe and how we are
to behave. Because the Bible carried God's message, it carries the same weight

---

[8]Bob E. Patterson, *Carl F. H. Henry* (Waco TX: Word Books, 1983) 117-19.

as if God were speaking to us personally. But to hear what God is saying to us, we must look at the Bible properly, and for this we need to rely on the internal working of the Holy Spirit to give us understanding, comprehension, and certainty of its truth. I do not have the ability to recognize meaning in the Bible without the help of the Holy Spirit. The Scripture (the objective word) and the Holy Spirit (the subjective inner illumination) constitute my authority as a believer.

THE DYNAMIC
NATURE OF
THE TRIUNE GOD

ERIC C. RUST
THE SOUTHERN BAPTIST THEOLOGICAL SEMINARY
LOUISVILLE KY 40280

Every Christian theological system must speak to the intellectual climate of its time. The Christian revelation must be interpreted in a way that both shows rational coherence and also speaks to the contemporary field of knowledge. This is why every great systematic theology possesses a philosophical cement and thereby builds a bridge to its world, provided such cement is consonant with some important strain of contemporary thinking. Thus we see Augustine using Neo-Platonism, Aquinas using Aristotle, Luther reflecting contemporary Occamism, and so on down to our own time. Barth, Brunner, Bultmann, Tillich, Macquarrie are respectively related to the philosophical thought of Kierkegaard, Buber and Heidegger. Moltmann and Pannenberg are likewise intimately bound up with the present currents of philosophical thinking.

Now one characteristic note of the thought of our time is the preoccupation with time. Modern thinkers take time seriously. This is very evident in the scientific area where the relativistic revolution of Einstein and its consequent cosmological speculation, the evolutionary understanding of the development of life initiated by Charles Darwin, and new quantum physical concerns of the new physics, have all enthroned the reality of time, change and becoming in our understanding of the natural universe. But then, ever since Hegel, an emphasis on time and change has initiated a new concern with history and the nature of historical thinking. Being has given place to becoming.

This shift of emphasis is particularly significant for Christian theology, for the Christian revelation is given in history and the testimony to it comes in a series of historical writings, our Bible. Furthermore, this biblical testimony is concerned with God as creator as well as redeemer, so that the findings of modern science are very relevant to the divine revelation to which the Bible testifies. The new historical thinking has provided a new understanding of the biblical revelation. It is recognized now by biblical scholarship that there is a historical movement in the divine unveiling, in which there is an interaction between this developing revelation and the cultural medium through which it is given. The biblical revelation becomes a dynamic reality, and God comes to us as a God who acts in history. Our historical time is a reality in the divine life and has its place in the divine purpose. At the center of this historical unveiling is Jesus of Nazareth, the incarnate presence of God in history. Here is the final assurance that our creaturely time is within the divine activity and has an eternal significance.

The movement in history of the Christian Church testifies to the divine unveiling as a continuing process in history. The original revelation to the Hebrew people and through Jesus Christ has been understood more deeply and made relevant to the new historical cultures that have emerged within the movement of historical time. In the early centuries of the Christian era, down indeed to the medieval period and beyond, the Greek cultural thought generally provided the medium through which the biblical revelation had to be expressed. This is already evident in our New Testament writings. In the centuries that followed, Neo-Platonism and Aristotelian modes of thought supplied the bridges through which theologians like Augustine and Thomas Aquinas made the Christian disclosure relevant to their own times. Greek thought, however, with its rationalism, has always tended to ignore the dynamic and historical aspect of the biblical revelation and to express its insights in a static form. The last two centuries, with the growing emphasis of the temporal framework of existence, have transferred the emphasis from the Greek concern with being to the Hebrew emphasis on becoming. The result can be a new and deeper understanding of the nature of God as Creator and Redeemer. This is the situation that we face today.

THE DIVINE ATTRIBUTES AND THE HISTORICITY OF GOD

In the earlier centuries until the Protestant Reformation, Christian theology was wedded to natural theology as its precursor, with the arguments for divine existence and attempts to establish some understanding of the divine nature upon natural evidence. Since the Reformation, this approach of natural theology has dropped into the background, and been ignored by some thinkers. It has more recently tended to be replaced by an emphasis on general revelation. At the present time, however, we are seeing a revived concern with theistic arguments and evidences. The classical differentiation was between the so-called metaphysical divine attributes and those more central understandings of the divine nature which come directly from the insights of the Christian revelation. This has still some degree of validity. Yet such "metaphysical attributes" are always associated with theistic philosophies, and theism as a viable religious philosophy has its roots initially in the biblical understanding of God. Such general theistic philosophical thinking should offer a background for understanding the nature of the God of Christian revelation. It can, indeed, provide some kind of intelligible bridge to the secular order.

In this essay, however, we shall concentrate upon the historical divine disclosure brought to a focus in Jesus the Christ. The so-called metaphysical attributes sometimes need to be modified in the light of this Christian revelation. Some are even invalid when applied to the biblical disclosure. When, however, they are applicable, they attain a much richer expression. As we shall see subsequently, the so-called divine attributes of impassibility, immutability, perfection as self-sufficiency, and timeless eternity are called in question or need modifying by the Christian revelation to which the biblical writings testify. Thus the divine disclosure both adjudges and confirms our philosophical questing. Actually the modification and even elimination of the attributes just referred to would make the Christian understanding more consonant with the preoccupation of contemporary thought with time and history. The Christian revelation then confirms secular questing and brings out its full significance.

In his painstaking investigation of the religious response to reality, Rudolf Otto identified this as an awareness of a mystery which both strikes fear and strangely attracts—a *mysterium tremendum et fascinans*. The deity is always a holy and awesome presence, a numinous being. The biblical revelation places such an understanding of God at the center of religious awareness. God is the holy one who inhabits eternity. Such holiness means separateness or apartness. God is other than his creatures.[1]

The biblical revelation increasingly gives to this holiness a moral content. God's holiness, as Isaiah declared, is bound up with his righteousness. God, in his lofty and enthroned splendor, is clothed in moral righteousness. His otherness is one of moral perfection. It is thus that he is separated from his creatures. He stands apart in his transcendent majesty and is characterized

---

[1]Rudolf Otto, *The Idea of the Holy,* trans. J. W. Harvey (Oxford: Oxford University Press, 1923) 220.

by moral purity and perfection. Thereby the Christian revelation confirms the philosophical questing which would postulate a God who embodies our human values. Yet the divine holiness warns us that such divine perfection is far removed from all human expressions of such values.

The Christian disclosure thus affirms a personal God. He is no rational pattern of universal ideas, as with Plato, no rational abstraction, as with Hegel, but personal being. He is will and purpose. He is mind and he knows. He is personal in the sense of purposive intelligence and reason. He is the living God, who acts, who creates, who enters into relationship with his creatures. His creatures do not have to argue to him as a static idea or an abstract ideal. They have to deal with him as a demanding presence. They can speak of his righteousness because he is personal. He acts in accord with his moral purpose.

We must, however, agree with many thinkers that we must not describe God as *a* person. As we shall see immediately, the trinitarian nature of God would seem to obviate this. He is personal mystery. At once we return to God's moral holiness, for in his transcendent perfection he stands apart from and above our human personal creatureliness. Yet this personal perfection does not isolate him in solitary splendor. One characteristic mark of human personality is the capacity for personal fellowship and relationship. The God of the biblical revelation manifests himself as this kind of personal being. He is uniquely beyond his creatures. He transcends them and yet their personal being points to his. They are made in his image, capable of living in fellowship with and responding to him.

Yet, if God is personal, he is also incorporeal. This is one aspect of what we mean by declaring that God is infinite. He is not a limited being, occupying a space, operating through a bodily structure. He is spaceless and not limited by any bodily structure. He is pure spirit. Mind is distinct from matter even though it emerged from the increasingly complex structures of physical energy by the evolutionary process. We can envisage self-conscious mind or spirit as existing apart from bodily structures, even though our finite minds operate within the limitations of such corporeality. God is infinite, unlimited, personal being. Any limitations that he has are self-imposed and self-created. Thus he accepts the limitations of the universe which he has created, comes to his creatures through it, and operates within the ordered structure which he has himself ordained. Our acceptance of miracle is a reminder that God is only limited by such ordered structure and laws if he so wills. The world is *not* his body. Yet he has chosen to reveal himself to us in, with, and under his created order and its creatures, especially personal beings like prophets and apostles. At the center of such activity is his incarnate presence within the humanity of Jesus the Christ.

This brings us to the focal point of the Christian revelation—the historicity of God. However we may seek to unveil this mystery, our faith is fundamentally a commitment to Jesus Christ as God's redemptive presence in the midst of our historical life. Here God has become man, and in this human guise, has borne our griefs and carried our sorrows. Jesus constitutes the humanity of God. In him God has lifted up our historical life and human experience into his own eternal existence. Here quite clearly we need to redefine the metaphysical attribute of God's eternity. God is not timeless being. Equally, however, eternity must not be identified with everlastingness. In the incarnation we know with certainty that our creaturely time has meaning in God's life. We cannot bar "becoming" from his being.

That time is within God's life does not mean that his time is the same as our time, but it does imply that becoming and even death are within his life. As Jüngel contends, the perishability of our temporal existence, the vanishing of the present with time's movement, was experienced by God in the humanity of Jesus.[2] Such, however, must not mean the death of God as Jüngel argues. Rather the death of Jesus is experienced in God as man experiences it. Following Moltmann we may say that the death of Jesus is not the death *of* God but death *in* God.[3] What we have in the incarnation is the disclosure of a God who is involved in the whole process of history and who in Jesus enters into engagement with our historical particularity. The incarnation, the historicity of God, brings to a focus and unveils that hidden and dynamic Presence behind all historical life. We know then that all our becoming is somehow in his being, that his being is continually coming into our becoming, that all our pasts are continually being judged, purified, and gathered into his ongoing life. This is the meaning of the cross and resurrection in which he overcomes our perishability and discloses himself as love. Here we can agree with Jüngel that "God has defined himself as Love on the Cross of Jesus."[4]

So we come to the reality of God as Love and return to a deeper consideration of the holy God. The divine holiness as characterized by righteousness and awe is the background of Otto's definition of the numinous as a mystery which both strikes fear and yet attracts. Our understanding of God as personal being, brought to focal disclosure in Jesus and his cross, shapes Otto's approach to the holy. A holy God meets us in two ways. The divine holiness has two aspects—a negative and a positive. It is both condemnatory

---

[2]See Eberhard Jüngel, *God as the Mystery of the World,* trans. Darrele L. Guder (Grand Rapids MI: William B. Eerdmans, 1983) especially 184-225.

[3]Jürgen Moltmann, *The Crucified God* (San Francisco: Harper and Row, 1985) 207.

[4]Jüngel, *God as the Mystery,* 220.

and redemptive. H. H. Farmer, in his analysis of personal relations as ana-
logues for the activity of a personal God, sees God approaching his creatures
as absolute claim and final succor. In his holy otherness, God meets us as
condemnation and, in our sin, we experience his presence as wrath. But he
is both a righteous God and a Savior. He who comes as righteous judge also
comes as redeemer. Indeed his judgment is always the underside of his love.
He gives his creatures over to their sins, yet in mercy pursues them into the
far country. This is the deep impact of the incarnation and the cross. His presence as wrath is yet the underside of grace. He judges but ever longs to communicate himself to his creatures. The holy God is essentially Love. God is
love, holy love.[5]

This kind of love is described by the Greek word *agape* in our New Testament. Nygren's insightful study of the Greek vocabulary for love has made
it clear that *eros* represents love in which the subject benefited also in satisfying the desire for the other person. It could be sensual but also a love that
was concerned with the well-being of the other. In the New Testament, however, a new word, *agape,* was coined and used especially of God. It was used
also as a gift of the Spirit to those committed to the Christ. Such love was
never self-regarding.[6] As Paul puts it in 1 Corinthians 13:5, *agape* does not
seek its own. It was other-regarding and was the love that God disclosed to
his creatures. It was grace and could define God's real being. The holy God
is this kind of love, the love that gives and spends itself, love that is other-
directed and not self-regarding. God *is* love. Such personal love is dynamic.
If God is "pure act" in Aristotle's sense of the word, he is not any unmoved
mover. To be the full essence of *agape* means that God is continually giving
himself. His goodness is always "spilling over." He is dynamic being.

THE TRIUNE GOD AND HIS CREATURES

The classical theologians declared that God is one and indivisible. This
divine attribute needs to be redefined in the light of the New Testament disclosure of the divine trinity. Already in the Old Testament testimony we can
see the preparation for such a disclosure in the emphasis on the divine Spirit
and on the Word of the Lord and the divine Wisdom. The early history of the
church is filled with the struggle to maintain the full personhood of the triune
God and to affirm the full deity of each person in the Godhead. It is not our
task here to delineate the various controversies and the misunderstandings as-

---

[5]H. H. Farmer, *The World and God* (London: Nesbit & Co., Ltd., 1955), especially 13-
31, and also *passim.*

[6]Anders Nygren, *Agape and Eros,* trans. Philip S. Watson (London: S.P.C.K., 1953).

sociated with *hypostasis, ousia* and *persona*. What does matter is that, in its great dogmatic creeds and definitions, the church affirmed the full unity of the Godhead and rejected any attempt to divide the triune God into three personal parts. Father, Son and Spirit were all equally and fully God and always participated fully in every divine act. This is very evident in the biblical testimony. In the divine act of creation the Divine Word or Son operates upon the primeval chaos and the Spirit of God hovers over the formless deep. When our Lord becomes incarnate, when the divine Word or Son takes flesh and becomes history, the Father speaks from heaven at his baptism and the Spirit comes down on him like a dove. Indeed, at his birth, the Spirit was there hovering over the womb of Mary.

The church sought to express this unity of action of the three persons and also their indivisibility into three distinct personal beings by using various expressions. They affirmed that the Son and the Spirit are of one substance with the Father. God is not three distinct substances. They held that the whole Godhead is present in each of the persons. Indeed, the three ''persons'' coinhere, interpenetrate, so that each includes the others. The ''persons'' are conjoined without any dividing medium and exist inseparably from one another.

The church early found itself caught between Scylla and Charybdis. On the one side, it would not opt for three gods, three centers of consciousness. Here the Cappadocian fathers were in danger, for they used three human beings as analogies for the Trinity, even though such tritheism was not in their intention. On the other side, there was the danger of postulating three successive modes of the divine activity. In this way of thinking, the Trinity was not applicable to the divine essence, God's innermost being. It was rather a description of the successive acts of the divine revelation, God's economy of disclosure, an economic trinity. Hence Sabellius was labelled as a heretic, and Patripassianism was proscribed. The church would have nothing to do with an attempt to crucify the Father and put the Holy Spirit to flight. In some way, the three manifestations of God's presence were indications of what God eternally is in his divine essence.

The real danger lay, of course, in the unfortunate misunderstandings caused by the final Greek differentiation of *hypostasis* and *ousia,* and the subsequent Latin employment of the word *persona*. This word did not at all mean *person* in our modern sense but was used to describe a mode or the role of an actor. Thus the modern meaning of ''person'' does not apply to the historic formulation of trinitarian dogma. Despite the disrepute into which modalistic Sabellianism placed the description ''mode,'' it would seem that this word might best describe the innermost being of God, provided we add the qualifying adjective ''eternal.''

Augustine attempted this approach and was evidently fearful of giving *persona* any sense of individual center of consciousness or personality. Over against the Cappadocian fathers, he used individual human analogies to describe the divine essence and likened the three persons to the one personal mind knowing itself, in the sense of *memoria* (the contents of the mind), *intelligentia* (the act of thinking), and *voluntas* (the will)—memory intelligence, and will in the act of self-reflection. This psychological analogy has its dangers for these three acts are within the self, and we are left, if it is pressed, with four rather than three—the Godhead and the three persons. We are reminded of the story of the woman visiting Trinity College at the University of Oxford. She noticed four images on the roof of one of the buildings and inquired of a passing Fellow what they represented. His reply was "Madam, that is the Holy Trinity." "Oh!" she said, "but then there should be only three." "Not at all," came the reply. "One God and three persons." Leaving this analogy on one side, we find that Barth advocates "mode of being" for "person" and that Rahner prefers to use "way of existing."

There are, of course, modern theologians like William Temple and Leonard Hodgson who prefer to follow the direction of the Cappadocians and describe God's innermost being as social, with the three persons as three centers of consciousness bound together in love.[7] One immediate value of this approach is that it does express immediately the essential being of God as Love. God is, within himself, a blessed society of self-giving love in which the three persons coinhere and interpenetrate in such a mysterious way that he is one and acts always in indivisible unity. One danger would be that this divine society might be such a structure of mutual self-giving that there would be no creative and self-giving urge to move beyond itself. The other danger, of course, is tritheism. This analogy does, as just suggested, preserve the dynamic nature of God as *agape*-love. Actually Augustine did use a personal analogy that preserved this when he used the threefold idea of the lover, the object loved and the love that unites them. This leans towards the social view.

The psychological analogy emphasizes the divine unity at the expense of plurality, and the social analogy emphasizes the reverse of this. The truth would lie between the two. All analogies serve but to point. Alan Richardson leans back on Augustine's analogy just cited above. He writes: "God is not a lonely God, but from all eternity possesses the Eternal Son as the object of his love."[8]

We are left with the mystery of the divine tri-unity as a dynamic personal presence of creative and self-giving love. We are dealing with the mysterious hiddenness of divine presence. God is known only as he chooses to make himself known. Any analogies we choose cannot finally unveil his mystery.

---

[7]William Temple. *Christus Veritas* (London: Macmillan, 1980) 276-85.

[8]Alan Richardson, *Faith, Science, Mystery* (Oxford: Oxford University Press, 1950) 144.

He is always the *deus absconditus,* the mysterious God of Abraham, Isaac and Jacob, not the rationally defined being of philosophical speculation, as Pascal pointed out. This, however, is not, as we have seen, to discount many metaphysical insights.

All this means that the biblical disclosure knows God as transcendent mystery even though he is also immanent in his world and discloses something of himself within it. We might come to some understanding of God's triune nature on this basis. We could envision God the Father as the transcendent depth of divine being out of which God utters himself in his eternal "mode of being" or "way of existence" as Word or Son—in the credal statement, the Son is eternally begotten or eternally generated, not made. As Word or Son, God acts creatively and redemptively, calling the universe and his creatures into being and redeeming them out of that nothingness into which they lapse and out of which they were called. Finally, as Spirit, God indwells his creation and moves it to respond to his creative and redemptive challenge through his Word. In this way, the trinity of divine love functions within the created order as the Father comes forth in the divine mode of Son and responds to himself as Spirit—a mutual communion of love that creates the creatures, sustains and redeems them. We have a dynamic universe that is pervaded by the divine presence.

Because God is *agape*-love, he is always giving himself so that creativity is consonant with his innermost nature. He is a Creator God, and yet he does not create for his own satisfaction. His love far transcends our human love, for it is never self-regarding. Furthermore, because he is, in himself, a blessed communion of love, he does not create out of any necessity. He is self-sufficient, as metaphysicians also usually require of deity. The creation of the world in no way completes his being. We can overcome the apparent contradiction here when we remember that the personal God of the biblical disclosure is completely free and unlimited, except that he always acts in ways consistent with his being as love. Hence he does not create out of any constraint to find fulfillment, for he has such in his own being. But he freely chooses to create that he may share his inner bliss with his creatures. In our finest moments we can do good to others without expectations of reward, and this might point a little towards the mystery of creation. Yet even our altruism does carry some moral satisfaction, so that even this analogy must not be pressed too far. The mystery of the divine motivation in creation lies hidden in God's perfect self-sufficiency of love, with his total altruism and his absolute freedom.

The mystery of divine creation involves the Christian insight that God creates the world out of nothing. This *creatio ex nihilo* affirms God's freedom from all limitations external to his own being and emphasizes the utter dependence upon God of all created things. As J. S. Whale puts it: "The doctrine of creation out of nothing is not a cosmological theory, but an expression of our adoring sense of the transcendent majesty of God, and of our utter dependence upon him.''[9] Indeed, Schleiermacher held that such absolute dependence upon God is the heart of man's religious response.[10]

The biblical disclosure requires us to see a high and noble purpose behind the divine creative act. The whole creative process is directed to the making of man in divine image, a finite being capable of responding freely to God's love and living in accord with the divine will. Thus man is created out of God's freely self-giving love to reflect back that love to his creator and share in the divine bliss. That man is created free to choose such a form of existence raises questions for God's management of his creation.

It must be emphasized that creation is a continuing process, a dynamic movement of the divine will in relation to his world. Creation is a process, as the biblical stories of creation make clear. Furthermore, the created order is continuously sustained by God, dependent on his will to sustain it in existence over the abyss of nothingness from which he has called it. This view of creation is perfectly consonant with the cosmological and evolutionary theories of modern science.

The Christian thinker cannot be satisfied with any deistic suggestion that God started the universe going, provided it with ordering laws and left it to move on its own. Rather he must postulate an immanent presence of God within the process itself, continuously active. Thus by challenging Word and creative Spirit, we must think of a dynamic presence of the triune God in converse with his creation. Hidden always behind and within the created process, God is yet actively evoking new responses and persuasively urging the process towards the goal of his purpose. Regin Prenter, interpreting Luther's thought, has echoed this understanding: ''The Son is the Word by which that which is created is brought forth from nothing. The Spirit is the sanctifying and preserving love of God by which he takes creation into himself and preserves it in the Word.''[11] The Word embodies the divine intention and purpose and, as such, brings the divine transcendence into creative and redemptive activity. The divine presence in the Spirit pervades the whole created order, permeating the whole universe with his presence and determining every atom

----

[9]J. S. Whale, *Christian Doctrine* (Cambridge: Cambridge University Press, 1942) 32.

[10]F. Schleiermacher, *The Christian Faith,* ed. H. R. Mackintosh and J. S. Stewart (Edinburgh: T. & T. Clark, 1948) 12ff. Consult E. C. Rust, *Positive Religion in a Revolutionary Time* (Philadelphia: Westminster Press) 35-46. Also, Richard Reinhold Niebuhr, *Schleiermacher on Christ and Religion* (New York: Charles Scribner's Sons, 1964) 108-34.

[11]Regin Prenter, *Spiritus Creator,* trans. J. M. Jensen (Philadelphia: Muhlenberg Press, 1953) 192.

and motion. Here we have the immanence of God.[12] Thus in his transcendence and immanence, creation is an act of the triune God, who calls into being, brings into full response and sustains created beings within his purpose.

In this way, we may understand what is meant by the divine attribute of omnipresence. The triune God is dynamically present throughout his universe. Yet we may also speak of his omnilocation, for he can bring his presence to a focus in a specific situation. He is free to locate his creative and sustaining presence. We may think of the immanent creator Spirit as organizing and guiding the natural process from within until, at long last, finite spirit may emerge within the process, with all the possibilities of free personal being. This writer likes John V. Taylor's description of the Holy Spirit as the ''Go-between-God,'' the cementing presence which holds the natural wholes together and sustains them. He writes: ''As a believer in the Creator Spirit I would say that deep within the fabric of the universe, therefore, the Spirit is present as the Go-Between who confronts each isolated spontaneous particle with the beckoning reality of the larger whole and so compels it to relate to others in a particular way; and that it is he who at every place lures the inert organisms forward by giving an inner awareness and recognition of the unattained.''[13] Many decades ago, C. E. Raven spoke of the Spirit as the *nisus* of the causality of the universe, ''the principle not only of its continuity but of its emergent novelty.''[14] Thus the Spirit may be defined as the holistic principle which is everywhere active and effective.[15] He moves the process towards ever more integrated wholes and ultimately to man—a creative cement!

If Paul could define the incarnation as a *kenosis* of the eternal Word (Philippians 2:6-8), we may also describe the hidden presence of the Spirit in the created process as a *kenosis*. H. W. Robinson suggested that the Spirit has truly accepted the limitations of the natural order, at all levels, in order to exercise his creative and directive activity. He argued that *kenosis* always means ''self-emptying and humiliation of spirit when it expresses itself, as it must, in 'degrees of reality' lower than itself.''[16] Thus, the spiritual must always ''lay aside some of its own attributes and powers when clothing itself

---

[12]H. F. Van Dusen, *Spirit, Son and Father* (New York: Charles Scribner's Sons, 1958) 177.

[13]John V. Taylor, *The Go-Between God* (London: SCM Press, 1978) 31.

[14]C. E. Raven, *Experience and Interpretation,* vol. 2 of *Natural Religion and Christian Theology* (Cambridge: Cambridge University Press, 1953) 144.

[15]Raven, *Experience,* 155.

[16]H. W. Robinson, *The Christian Experience of the Holy Spirit* (London: Nisbet and Co., Ltd., 131) 87.

in the material.''[17] We might express this by suggesting that the Spirit always accepts the limitations of creaturely being within which it is operative. This would help us to understand why scientific analysis and method can provide a descriptive explanation of natural phenomena at their own level without any reference to the divine presence.

As we move from the process of nature to the movement of history, the Spirit accepts our personal freedom and accommodates himself to our human lot and its consequences. The final disclosure in the incarnation opens up a new access to human lives. With the Christ the Spirit enters into a conscious indwelling in those who open their lives to his presence and surrender their freedom to his loving direction. Thus the church becomes the body of Christ, the society of those in whose hearts the Christ dwells by faith through his Spirit. The incarnate Word continues his work through the indwelling Spirit. Since the Word or the Cosmic Christ is ever the vehicle of divine disclosure, dare we not say that wherever men perceive the divine light and open their lives to it, the Spirit does also become a conscious and indwelling presence.

THE DIVINE OMNIPOTENCE AND THE ETERNAL CROSS

Our discussion of the divine immanence in the created order as creative, sustaining and redemptive presence requires a careful definition of the nature of such a controlling presence. To say that God is a dynamic presence concerned to achieve his purpose in creation means to understand what his power is. To declare, as the biblical testimony does, that he will achieve his purpose implies the divine omnipotence. He is in control of his world. Immediately, however, we face the issue of evil in many forms—natural evil within the process of nature and moral evil in man's mishandling of his freedom and its consequences for himself and his fellows. Earthquakes, volcanoes, tornadoes, hurricanes, floods are part of our natural heritage. Disease, germs and bacillae we share with the animal order. Even the dread disease of cancer did not begin with the emergence of man. The ills and perversions of the human body are not peculiar to humanity but present in all life. What is peculiar to human history are the evil intentions of individuals and societies and the pain and suffering that they visit upon their fellows. It is one thing to speak of the created process as directed to a divinely intended perfection, but, on the way, it has spawned many evils and been attended by much suffering. Like Tennyson in the poem ''In Memoriam,'' we are repelled by it all and wonder where God is: we too ''falter where [we] firmly trod, and falling with [our] weight of cares upon the world's great altar stairs, that slope thro' darkness

---

[17]Ibid.

up to God, [we] stretch lame hands of faith, and grope . . . and faintly trust the larger hope.'' But we do hope! We have to build on God's nature as love.

Modern science is making us increasingly aware that the created process has a mixture of order and contingency, law and chance. On the one hand, we have randomness and contingencies. Random mutations play their part in the evolutionary development of the species. Below the organisms, in the atomic and sub-atomic world, at the very basis of the physical energy, we have indeterminacy and acausality. On the other hand, at the root of the creative process, we have developing regularities, the ''laws of nature,'' which are statistical and yet express the average and expected behavior of the natural order. These constitute that framework of orderliness which allows us to speak of the natural *order*. They are the habitual forms of behavior, ingredient in the created energy, and become evident at the various levels of complexity in which that energy becomes patterned or knotted up. Under the immanent guidance of the divine Spirit, there emerge life, mind and spirit. The whole process is thus subject to the presence of a law-like framework. yet within this there are the elements of randomness, contingency, and indeterminacy, which the divine Creator introduced into and sustains in the process. They make possible those mutations which serve to elicit the potencies for life, consciousness and self-conscious mind or spirit which are latent in the stream of energy by the creative intention of God.

We can understand something of the mystery of their presence, if we remember the divine intention to create free beings who shall be free to respond to the creator's love. A world was being shaped on our planet with sufficient openness and unfinishedness for free and creative human beings to live and operate within it, when they emerged at the appropriate point in the process. We might expect flexibility within the framework of orderliness. We can say that the world has not come as a fixed and determined structure. Rather it has come as an open and unfinished order, that it may serve God's purpose. This is a world in the making, and the making of humankind is its object.

Austin Farrer makes an illuminating comment: ''The purpose of a machine is to deliver the goods. What goods would a cosmic machine deliver, and to whom? Might the Creator have thought to glory himself by constructing a cosmic gramophone, streamlined for the production of symphonic Alleluias? But that it not how, it seems, he thought to glorify himself, and he is wise.''[18]

We can see in all this the activity of the Creator Spirit, sustaining even the divagations, the unexpectedly evil and unaesthetic twists which nature

---

[18]Austin Farrer, *Love Almighty and Ills Unlimited* (Garden City NY: Doubleday and Co., Inc., 1961) 55.

produces in its fecundity, and which are present in the pain and suffering that underlie the upward surge of the process. Most of all, we can see the divine sustaining of human freedom with its selfish waywardness and sinful willing. We can say this because, in the case of the Creator, we are not dealing with invincible and irresistible force, but with self-giving and redemptive love. God's omnipotence is not seen in a force which brooks no opposition but in a persuasive restraint which woos his creatures until his goal is attained. Kierkegaard held that the distinctive quality of the divine omnipotence lies just in this capacity for withdrawing and letting be, leaving the creature free with a degree of independence. He wrote: "All finite power makes dependent, only omnipotence can make independent, can bring forth from nothing that which has continuance in itself by reason of the fact that omnipotence is withdrawn."[19] Irresistible compulsion gives place to constraining, persuasive love.

The Creator is limited only by his own self-chosen and self-created limitations—by the orders and regularities, the contingencies and human freedoms which he has called into being in his world. As Farrer says, this is the way of his wisdom, and we can adore the mystery of such love and grace. He could wipe the created order out, and start again in some other way. But he longs for creatures to share his love and respond to his loving presence. So he bears our suffering and evils, the travails of nature and the suffering and agonies, sins and perverted wills of historical human beings, that in the end his love may triumph.

Is not this what the *kenosis* of the Creator Spirit implies? The self-limitation of the creative Spirit carries the agony of creating and permitting an element of disorder and chance within order so that he may guide the whole to become a gathering of free and finite spirits. Paul therefore sees a groaning and travailing creation waiting for the unveiling of the sons of God and, within it, the indwelling Spirit himself groaning with groanings that cannot be uttered (Romans 8:19-24). This is the "Calvary" of the Spirit.

This "Calvary" of the Spirit in the process of nature reaches its climax in the movement of history when the creative and redemptive Word takes human form and brings the suffering and redeeming love of God to a climax on Calvary's hill. The *kenosis* of the Spirit is matched by the *kenosis* of the Word Incarnate. Here God lifts our historical life up into his own innermost being, bears our sins and carries our sorrows, that he may redeem the humanity which he has created. It is on Calvary that the triune God shows the nature of his omnipotent love, for beyond the Cross there was a resurrection morn and the assurance that divine love is triumphant over sin and evil and death. The Cross

---

[19]Søren Kierkegaard, *Christian Discourses,* trans. Walter Lowrie (London: Oxford University Press, 1939) 182n.

of Jesus is a window into the heart of God, and ''we shall expect to find fore-
shadowings of it at every preliminary stage of the creative process.''[20] Any
doctrine of creation and providence has a cross at its heart.

Such divine suffering is not an imperfection if we remember that it is vi-
carious. God does not suffer from the pain of guilt, for he is supreme goodness. In his self-sufficiency he does not suffer from the pain of loneliness. In
his perfect knowledge, there is no pain of fear. His suffering is a feeling with
his creatures, an identification manifested supremely in the incarnation. Here
is a mystery that passes our comprehension.

We cannot therefore speak of the impassibility of God. Indeed, we have
also to define carefully his immutability, and to refer it to his unfaltering purpose. Because God is personal and because he is love, we are not dealing with
an impersonal absolute or unmoved mover, a *deus philosophicum*. W. R.
Matthews wrote: ''The immutability of God, as religion conceives it, is more
like the steadfastness of a good man than the unalterable properties of a tri-
angle.''[21] We are speaking of God's faithfulness, his steadfast love. Our whole
Christian experience of God means that we cannot identify his immutability
with timelessness. The whole implication of his historicity in Jesus would imply this. He is unwavering in his steadfast love through all the vicissitudes of
our human history.

So we finish with the divine passibility. As Dean Inge once put it: ''The
good news of Christianity is that suffering is itself divine.''[22] Or more recently, we hear Bonhoeffer declare that ''only a suffering God can help.''[23]
The Cross is lifted into the heart of God. The divine suffering is brought to a
focus in the historicity of God himself on Calvary. What Christ did in his life
and death must be seen against the background of an eternal atonement in
which grace is ever triumphing over wrath. John Baillie contends that any
saving power finding its place in man's religious history is related to the Christ
event: ''I would . . . insist that the Eternal Christ who was made flesh in Jesus of Nazareth, and eternal atonement which was made *event* on Calvary,
were and are the source of every 'saving process' which has at any time proved
to be for the healing of the nations.''[24] His brother, Donald Baillie, penetrates
to the heart of divine passibility when he declares that ''the Atonement is

---

[20]Raven, *Experience*, 157.

[21]W. R. Matthews, *God in Christian Thought and Experience* (London: Nisbet and Co.,
Ltd., 1930) 255.

[22]W. R. Inge, *Speculum Animae* (London: Longmans Green and Co., 1920) 22.

[23]Dietrich Bonhoeffer, *Letters and Papers from Prison* (New York: The Macmillan Co.,
1962) 220.

[24]John Baillie, *The Sense of the Presence of God* (New York: Charles Scribner's Sons,
1962) 201-202.

something within the life of God, wrought by God Himself, and applied by him to men in every age.''[25] Mankind is living in the wilderness of its own mishandled freedom, confronted by the barred gate and flaming sword that shut it into its own judgment. Yet always, in the background, are the out-stretched arms of a divine love that cares, and suffers, and pursues until mankind forsakes its foolish ways and turns to God. The Cross is supra-temporal, in God's eternal being. The arms of love are outstretched on God's eternal Cross.

---

[25]Donald Baillie, *God Was in Christ* (London: Faber & Faber Ltd., 1948) 192.

THE MYSTERY
OF THE CROSS

FISHER HUMPHREYS
NEW ORLEANS BAPTIST THEOLOGICAL SEMINARY
NEW ORLEANS LA 70126

I

To alert observers of our world, it would seem that the crucifixion of Jesus by Roman soldiers was not a mystery. Was it not simply another in the long series of injustices inflicted by the powerful of this world upon the weak?

It was that, of course. And yet, from the beginning those who knew and remembered Jesus' cross thought of it in another way also. They proclaimed it as an element in the purpose of God. Thus Peter said both ''you killed him by letting sinful men crucify him,'' and ''in accordance with his own plan God had already decided that Jesus would be handed over to you'' (Acts 2:23, TEV).

In order to understand how the cross is both an act of human injustice (and thus in no sense a mystery) and also an element in the purpose of God (and thus a profound mystery), we must interpret the cross. We must see it as a divine act in the middle of human history. ''God was in Christ, reconciling the world unto himself'' (2 Corinthians 5:19).

But how can we interpret an act of God, even if it did occur in the middle of human history? Strictly speaking, God's nature and purpose and activities have no precise analogies in the world of our finite and sinful human experience. ''To whom can the holy God be compared? Is there anyone else like him?'' (Isaiah 40:25, TEV). The answer, of course, is that there is no one to whom God can be compared, for God is the only God.

And yet, in order to understand God, comparisons must be made. Finite realities must be pressed into service as metaphors for the infinite God. Human events must be made to serve as models for the divine event of the cross. In fact, there is good reason to believe that even before Jesus came, God had prepared some human realities to serve as metaphors for the great saving event of the cross.

II

We know that the earliest church interpreted the cross by using the realities of their previous experience as metaphors. Nor were they making a virtue of necessity, for they really believed that the cross was a saving act of God, and they also really believed that it was the ultimate fulfillment of many of the practices, concepts, hopes, and other realities which had been theirs before Christ arrived. It was not the case that they saw the cross only as an act of human injustice and the resurrection as an act of God; rather, from the beginning they said that ''Christ died for our sins'' as well as that God raised Jesus on the third day, as the classic passage on the apostolic preaching makes clear (1 Corinthians 15:1-7). And also from the beginning, they were confident that both his death and his resurrection were ''according to the Scriptures''; that is, both Christ's death and his resurrection were bringing to fulfillment much that was written in the Hebrew Bible. From the beginning the church believed that the cross was a saving act of God; they proclaimed that fact to others; and they interpreted the mystery of God's act by using metaphors from their Scriptures.

Some of their metaphors were drawn from quite general Jewish contexts. The two principal ones were the eschatological and the cultic. In the context of Israel's hope that God would act in a mighty way to inaugurate a new age of freedom, justice, peace, and forgiveness, Peter preached at Pentecost that in fact God's act had just occurred; the two great signs of the new age, resurrection and the gift of the Spirit, had clearly taken place, and so divine forgiveness was available to all who accepted the message about Christ.

The cultus of Israel provided the early church with several metaphors for the death of Christ. Christ is the ultimate high priest (Hebrews 4:14-5:10). He is the Passover lamb (1 Corinthians 5:7). His blood is the blood of Yom Kippur, only more perfect and final (Hebrews 9:6-14). He has made a new covenant between God and man by his blood (1 Corinthians 11:25). That covenant is now operative because, like a human will, it took effect when its author died (in Greek, the work *diathekes* means either ''will'' or ''covenant''; see Hebrews 9:16-18).

Other metaphors for the cross were drawn from more specific contexts. For example, Jesus was the Son of Man who suffered for his faithful witness to God, and who was finally vindicated by God.[1] Similarly, Jesus was the person of whom the Psalmist spoke, who in his great troubles cried out to God for help and who, when God had helped him, gathered his friends together for a *Todah* in which he sang praise to God for his help.[2] Again, Jesus was the Servant of the Lord who accepted the punishment due others in order to provide healing and forgiveness for them (Isaiah 52:12-53:12; Acts 8:26-35). Again, because Jesus died upon a tree, he died under a curse, and thus he provided deliverance for those who live under the curse of trying unsuccessfully to be fully obedient to the Torah (see Deuteronomy 27:26, Galatians 3:13, 10).

Many other Old Testament realities serve as metaphors for the mystery of the cross. Perhaps the most brief is the single word *exodon* in Luke 9:31. Moses and Elijah spoke to Jesus of his exodus, his death, which, like the Exodus from Egypt long before, is a mighty act of God which provides liberation for his people. It is salutary to reflect on the fact that Luke provided in a single word a "theory of atonement," that is, a model for understanding the meaning of the cross.

III

I do not know how many metaphors for the mystery of the cross appear in the New Testament, but I suspect there are at least twenty. But the interpretation of the cross did not end with the New Testament. Through the centuries Christians have sought in contexts familiar to themselves other metaphors for the cross. For example, the early Christians of Alexandria were very concerned with human mortality, and they saw Christ as providing immortality by uniting mortal human nature to his immortal divine nature.[3] In the medieval period, Anselm saw the cross as the satisfaction of the honor of God, a metaphor whose contexts were the feudal and penitential systems. John Calvin's theory of substitutionary punishment also has the penitential system as a presupposition; to those who were attempting to pay for their sins by pen-

---

[1]This interpretation was given by C. F. D. Moule in *The Origin of Christology* (Cambridge: Cambridge University Press, 1977) 11-22.

[2]This interpretation of the cry of dereliction was given by James L. Mays in "Prayer and Christology: Psalm 22 as Perspective on the Passion," *Theology Today* 42:3 (October, 1985) 322-331.

[3]Paul Tillich suggested that the fathers of the church were preoccupied with mortality, the reformers with personal guilt, and modern man with meaninglessness; see *The Courage To Be* (New Haven: Yale University Press, 1951) 40-63.

ances, Calvin offered the wonderful news that Jesus had already paid it all. P. T. Forsyth and others maintained the same message in a context of morality rather than law, by emphasizing the atoning value of Christ's obedience. H. R. Mackintosh, D. M. Baillie, Leonard Hodgson, and others, working in the context of interpersonal relationships, saw the suffering of Christ as God's acceptance of the costliness of forgiving those who had wronged him.[4]

A fascinating proposal was made by Don Richardson in his book *Peace Child*. After failing by the use of biblical metaphors to communicate the gospel to a pre-literate tribe of people called Sawi on Netherlands New Guinea, he employed as a metaphor for Christ's work an event of their experience, namely, the permanent exchange of children by warring tribes for the purpose of making peace. The result was that the Sawi understood the gospel and eventually accepted it. Richardson proposed that "redemptive analogies" are to be found in all cultures, and that God expects his people to locate and employ them.[5]

The diverse metaphors which the later church employed for interpreting the cross were not intended to displace the metaphors found in the Bible. On the contrary, later writers have attempted to re-present the biblical view in metaphors familiar in non-biblical cultures.

C. S. lewis made a proposal concerning metaphors which is relevant here. He wrote of the importance of both teacher's metaphors and pupil's metaphors.[6] In the Bible God provided us with his teacher's metaphors for the cross. But many Christians, as students trying to interpret the cross, have employed metaphors from their own cultures, all the while believing fully and completely in the truth of the authorized biblical metaphors.

IV

The New Testament contains diverse teachings about the person of Christ. Challenges from Arius, Apollinaris, and Nestorius compelled the church of the fourth and fifth centuries to prescribe certain formulas for speaking about Christ; henceforth he was to be understood as one person having two natures without division or confusion, and so on. The Nicene Creed and the Chalcedonian Definition provided permanent, fixed points for the thinking of the church concerning the person of Christ.

---

[4]I discussed several of the later metaphors in Chapter Three of *The Death Of Christ* (Nashville: Broadman Press, 1978).

[5]Don Richardson, *Peace Child* (Ventura CA: Regal Books, 1974) 288.

[6]C. S. Lewis, *Rehabilitations and Other Essays* (Oxford: Oxford University Press, 1939) 140-41.

In contrast to this, the universal church never prescribed fixed points for thinking about the work of Christ, even though the New Testament, as we have seen, contains a similar diversity of teachings concerning the cross. In this, I am confident, the church has acted wisely. The result is that the church has maintained a variety of complementary interpretations of the cross. This posture of variety may be as close as we can come to doing justice both to the various New Testament metaphors and to the fact that the cross, an act of God, is a mystery with no exact analogy in human experience. A wonderful advantage of the absence of a single authorized metaphor for the cross is that those who attempt to communicate the gospel—the message of which the cross is the center—always have access to many metaphors as they attempt to preach to people of diverse cultures and experiences.

This leads us to the question of the function of metaphors for the cross. What do people use the metaphors for? What are they attempting to achieve, as they speak of the cross in these various ways?

One obvious answer, which we have just been observing, is that people interpret the cross in order to inform, persuade, and attract people to Christian commitment. For example, Philip spoke to the Ethiopian about Jesus as the Suffering Servant in order to bring the Ethiopian to faith. Calvin spoke of Christ as punished for our sins in order to open up to people who lived under the penitential system the option of trusting Christ for complete forgiveness. Don Richardson spoke to the Sawi about Christ as God's peace child in order to evangelize the Sawi. In our age of unbelief, Jürgen Moltmann has argued that the cross requires us to revise our understanding of God, to see God not as impassible but as suffering, because only a suffering God is credible to people today.[7]

A second function of metaphors for the cross concerns praxis rather than faith. The cross has been interpreted in order to authorize social changes, both ecclesiastical and socio-political. For example, the writer of Hebrews argued that since Christ died as a final sacrifice for sins, it was not only superfluous but disloyal for Christians to return to Jerusalem for the Jewish sacrifices. Since it was by no means self-evident what posture the church ought to take toward the Jewish cultus (Jesus never withdrew from the Temple; also, see Acts 21:26, 1 Corinthians 9:20-23), the argument of the book of Hebrews may well have been shocking to many in the early church. Of course, with hindsight later Christians saw that the writer was indeed correct, and that God was leading the church away from its early status as a special sect of Judaism.

A recent example of developing an interpretation of the cross to authorize social change is found in the work of Jon Sobrino. He argued that the cross

---

[7]Jürgen Moltmann, *The Crucified God* (London: SCM Press, 1973).

can be properly understood as an act with both religious and political implications. Jesus was crucified by the Romans for political insurrection, at the instigation of Jews whose reasons were more religious than political. This fact, he saw, demands that Christians participate in activities of political liberation.[8]

Both the evangelistic and praxis functions of interpretation of the cross are important, even indispensable, if the church is to carry out its mission task. I want now to suggest that interpretations of the cross have a third function. It may seem a timid function compared to the others, but I believe it is an important one.

Interpretations of the cross fulfill a deep human need to understand, a need which exists in us naturally and which is intensified by our faith in Christ. Theology is *fides quaerens intellectum;* better yet, it is *caritas quaerens intellectum.* The quest to understand, to appreciate and internalize and deepen one's grasp of the cross, is not a luxury to be relinquished in deference to evangelism or praxis. It too is an authentic function of faith. Spirituality and theology are closely related.[9] Those who are devoted want to understand; their devotion helps them to understand; yet as their understanding deepens, the mystery of the cross deepens even more. When faith seeks to understand the mystery of the cross, it ends up "lost in wonder, love, and praise."

---

[8]Jon Sobrino, *Christology at the Crossroads* (Maryknoll NY: Orbis Books, 1978) 179-236.

[9]Hans Urs von Balthasar, "The Unity of Theology and Spirituality," *Convergences To the Source of Christian Mystery* (San Francisco: Ignatius Press, 1983) 17-45.

HERMENEUTICS, THEOLOGY, AND THE HOLY SPIRIT

LARRY HART
ORAL ROBERTS UNIVERSITY
TULSA OK 74171

"The dissolution of the traditional doctrine of Scripture constitutes a crisis at the very foundation of modern Protestant theology."[1] Thus, Wolfhart Pannenberg expressed succinctly the present state of modern theology in relation to the authority and interpretation of the Bible. Both David Tracy and Gerhard Ebeling in their treatments of theological methodology have corroborated this verdict.[2] Indeed, the word "crisis" seems manifestly appropriate both in view of the chaotic pluralism of our day and the apparent divine judgment (compare the Greek *krisis*) on the impotence of much modern theology.

The issue of the Bible's authority and meaning has clearly become a virtual Rubicon among contemporary theologians. One either adheres to the classical concept of an authoritative biblical revelation or chooses to redefine the Bible's authority in functional terms (or jettison the concept altogether) with the result that a gangrenous "unsound doctrine" (see 2 Timothy 2:17; 4:3f) has eaten away at the very life of the church. Clark Pinnock is correct

---

[1]Wolfhart Pannenberg, *Basic Questions in Theology*, 2 vols., trans. George H. Kehm (Philadelphia: Fortress Press, 1970) 1:4.

[2]See David Tracy, *Blessed Rage for Order: The New Pluralism in Theology* (New York: Seabury Press, 1975) 4, where he refers to the "crisis of the Christian theologian in the modern world," in his chapter, "The Pluralist Context of Contemporary Theology," 3-21. Ebeling also sees a "crisis in orientation": Gerhard Ebeling, *The Study of Theology*, trans. Duane A. Priebe (Philadelphia: Fortress Press, 1978) 1.

when he asserts that the "crisis of the Scriptures is in fact the crisis of Christian theology itself and the cause of the deepest polarization of all in the churches."[3]

Langdon Gilkey has argued that the "present crisis" exists because the results of modern science and biblical criticism have simply made it impossible for many contemporary theologians to accept biblical authority any longer.[4] Ed Farley and Peter Hodgson concur that the "consensus [on the Scripture principle] seems to be falling apart."[5] And Wolfhart Pannenberg has aptly summarized the situation by referring to the "double crisis" of (1) historical criticism and (2) the hermeneutical problem which threatens Christian theology at present.[6]

Evangelicals, longtime champions of the Protestant Scripture principle, have come to realize more clearly than ever that a recovery of the Bible's authority is only a half-solution. The battle of the 1980s centers around hermeneutical issues related to how we have access to and how we apply the teachings of Scripture. A whole new battery of questions has emerged as to how the meaning of any literary document is ascertained. What is becoming increasingly evident is that the disciplines of biblical exegesis, biblical theology, systematic theology, and homiletics each struggle with "hermeneutical" problems, the solutions to which appear to be strikingly similar and integrally related.

Perhaps the greatest need at this juncture is simply to gain a broader perspective on the issues and to recognize a few pointers in what seems to be the right direction. Therefore, after an initial exploration into the hermeneutical nature of theology we shall look in turn at philosophical hermeneutics, evangelical hermeneutics, charismatic hermeneutics, and the future prospects of theology in relation to hermeneutics.

THE HERMENEUTICAL NATURE OF THEOLOGY

The term "hermeneutics" has proven to be notoriously slippery in modern usage. Initially it referred simply to the methods of arriving at the meaning of a given text in its original historical, literary, and cultural context. More

---

[3]Clark H. Pinnock, *The Scripture Principle* (San Francisco: Harper & Row, 1984) xv.

[4]Langdon Gilkey, *Naming the Whirlwind: The Renewal of God-Language* (New York: The Bobbs-Merrill Co., 1969) 73ff.

[5]Edward Farley and Peter C. Hodgson, "Scripture and Tradition," in *Christian Theology: An Introduction to Its Traditions and Tasks,* ed. Peter C. Hodgson and Robert H. King (Philadelphia: Fortress Press, 1982) 35.

[6]Pannenberg, *Basic Questions,* 12. Pannenberg argues for a theology of revelation based on universal history rather than a return to biblical authority, however.

recently interest has focused on the historical and cultural limitations of the *interpreter* seeking to derive meaning from the text. The term has also been expanded accordion-like to encompass the historical and literary tools themselves and perhaps stretched to the breaking point to encompass biblical and systematic theology in their entirety.

This tendency toward "skidding around on an increasingly broad semantic field"[7] is unfortunate, but it has served the purpose of pointing up the similarities of problems encountered in each of the various theological disciplines. Specifically, I want to highlight how the hermeneutical challenges of biblical studies, systematic theology, and preaching run parallel.

Krister Stendahl's now classic article on the nature of biblical theology did not prove to be the last word on the subject, but it did serve the purpose early on of highlighting the significance of historical distance expressed in the separate programmatic questions, "what it meant" and "what it means."[8] Biblical exegesis by the use of historical and literary methods has sought to explicate objectively and descriptively the original meaning of the scriptural texts. The biblical expositor in turn has addressed the question of the contemporary significance and application based on the controlling results of precise exegesis. That has been the ideal held forth. Philosophical hermeneutics has introduced vexing questions (to be referred to later) that have complicated the situation, but the basic approach of relating the past "horizon" to the present one remains.

Interestingly, systematic theologians are faced with virtually the same challenge. They seek effective means of relating the Christian faith and the teachings of Scripture to modern questions and modern knowledge. Again, a bipolar reality is encountered: (1) the historical given of Scripture and the faith, and (2) the contemporary pole of the modern setting. Each pole must be examined separately, and then an attempt must be made to bring about a meaningful synthesis. The final product is a systematic theology. Moreover, this somewhat simplistic portrayal of the task of systematic theology is found to be strikingly similar to the preacher's task.[9]

To the preachers falls the exciting, creative, and yet often agonizing task of effectively relating the Bible's teachings to the present-day needs and questions of their listeners. They stand "between two worlds," to echo the

---

[7]D. A. Carson, "Hermeneutics: A Brief Assessment of Some Recent Trends," *Themelios* 4:2 (January 1980) 14.

[8]Krister Stendahl, "Biblical Theology, Contemporary," *IDB* 1:418-32.

[9]I always try to impress upon my students that their class notes in systematic theology should prove as helpful to them in their future sermon preparation as their notes from exegetical courses.

title of a recent excellent homiletics text.[10] They wrestle with their task until the walls which separate their own century from the first become transparent so that when Paul, for example, speaks, the contemporary person hears.[11]

From this distance it becomes clear that the church faces a fundamental hermeneutical problem. The field of biblical studies is in chaos because of a lack of consensus on key exegetical and hermeneutical issues. In turn, systematic theologians are divided on the resultant problems within their own discipline, and the preachers seeking the scholars' help have too often sounded an uncertain note.

Almost twenty years ago William Hordern put his finger on the problem in contemporary theology. He noted the emergence of two distinct groups of theologians. The ''transformers'' are those theologians who have concluded that modern man cannot possibly accept, as it stands, the classical Christian message rooted in Scripture. People have changed; and the Christian faith must be ''transformed'' if it is to survive. ''Translators,'' on the other hand, resist such drastic change and maintain that the message, if properly translated, still evinces a powerful relevance.[12]

Clark Pinnock began his service at McMaster Divinity College in Hamilton, Ontario by sounding a similar note.[13] In a most articulate way he set forth the fundamentally different approaches of ''classical (conservative, orthodox) theology'' and the ''liberal experiment.'' Again, a bi-polar model was employed. The instinct of classical theology is to put more weight on the side of the historic beliefs taught in Scripture. Contemporary knowledge and questions must simply bow before and adapt to the biblical norm. Theologians leaning strongly toward the contemporary pole feel the need to ''revise'' or ''reconstruct'' the faith in more palatable modern terms. The result is in many cases a virtually alien gospel. The liberal experiment has tended to compromise its fidelity to and continuity with the historic faith. The conservative approach has too often failed to respond creatively and authentically to the contemporary situation leaving the impression that a historic faith

---

[10]John R. W. Stott, *Between Two Worlds: The Art of Preaching in Twentieth Century* (Grand Rapids MI: William B. Eerdmans Publishers, 1982).

[11]Barth in his *Römerbrief* described Calvin's commentaries in these laudatory terms. Cited in F. F. Bruce, *Commentary on the Book of Acts, The New International Commentary on the New Testament* (Grand Rapids MI; William B. Eerdmans Publishers, 1954) 8f.

[12]William Hordern, *Introduction*, vol. 1 of *New Directions in Theology Today* (Philadelphia: Westminster Press, 1966) 136-54.

[13]An edited form of his address was subsequently published: Clark H. Pinnock, ''An Evangelical Theology: Conservative and Contemporary,'' *Christianity Today* 13:7 (5 January 1979) 23-29.

connotes an antiquated faith. Pinnock argues for a creative conservatism that is responsive to contemporary needs and problems.[14]

A virtual continental divide has emerged. The liberal consensus within mainline Christianity has, in effect, compromised biblical authority. Their biblical scholars can no longer discern a univocal, or at least unified, message from Scripture. Their theologians have "revised" the faith to the point that its transforming power seems to have been lost. Their preachers too often lack an authoritative "thus saith the Lord!" At the same time, there seems to be an apparent revival of orthodoxy. Conservatives have begun to do their homework on almost every front. Their biblical scholars are as confident in Scripture and its clear message as ever. Their theologians have begun to venture their own systematic statements.[15] And their preachers increasingly evince impressive exegetical and expositional skills. Their churches, on the whole, seem to show healthy growth and increased activism.

Why do we see this seeming bifurcation within modern Christianity? Many would trace the roots of liberal theology back to Friedrich Schleiermacher, (1768-1834), who responded to the tumultuous changes within western civilization with his own unique hermeneutical approach to the theological task.

PHILOSOPHICAL HERMENEUTICS

Pinnock highlights the "cultural shift to secular modernity beginning in the Renaissance, and to rationalist modernity, brought on by the Enlightenment, and the liberal response to it."[16] Clearly, the enthronement of reason and the erosion of biblical authority through destructive biblical criticism precipitated the departure of many from classical orthodoxy. And yet, it was the desire to salvage the faith that prompted Schleiermacher to strike out on a new path.

Not able to embrace traditional theological categories and yet repulsed by the rationalism of his colleague at the University of Berlin, George W. F.

---

[14]Ibid. Clearly in the same tradition, Millard J. Erickson argues for an evangelical "contemporizing" of the Christian message in submission to the Bible's authority. See his *Christian Theology*, 3 vols. (Grand Rapids MI: Baker Publishing House, 1983) 1:ch.5.

[15]Carl F. H. Henry's six-volume magnum opus, *God, Revelation and Authority* (Waco: Word Books, 1976-1983) will perhaps serve as the standard conservative treatment of prolegomena, biblical authority, and the doctrine of God for years to come. Millard Erickson's three-volume *Christian Theology* has already been mentioned. A number of other leading scholars will be mentioned later. My own mentor, Dale Moody—except for his somewhat "uncritical" acceptance of modern science and biblical criticism (at least he has refused to bury his head in the sand!)—has published his widely-acclaimed evangelical summa, *The Word of Truth: A Summary of Christian Doctrine Based on Biblical Revelation* (Grand Rapids MI: William B. Eerdmans Publishers, 1981). Few have achieved a comparable synthesis.

[16]Pinnock, *The Scripture Principle*, xiii.

Hegel (1770-1831), Schleiermacher, in effect, drew upon his pietistic roots to construct an approach to theology based on religious feeling. He chose to downplay the doctrinal and ethical dimensions of the faith and to build upon the religious dimensions of God-consciousness'': (1) the feeling of absolute dependence upon God, (2) the experience of sin and guilt, and (3) the experience of grace. He approached his task in a very sophisticated manner so as to recommend the Christian faith to the ''cultured despisers'' of Berlin society.

Schleiermacher's philosophical liberalism became evident in his approach to the doctrine of revelation. The reality and truth of God emerge from within us rather than being bestowed upon us from without, according to Schleiermacher. Thus, theology is simply the very human endeavor of working out the implications of this common religious experience. There is no authoritative truth revealed from God in an infallible Bible, for example.

In terms of hermeneutics, a topic in which he was extremely interested, Schleiermacher dealt with issues that are very much to the fore today. He argued that a certain ''preunderstanding,'' moving from the known to the unknown, was necessary to grasp the meaning of a text, along with a ''self-understanding'' which enables one to empathize, as it were, with the text. His jettisoning of biblical authority as traditionally understood, and his emphasis on the importance of considering the present horizon in the hermeneutical circle give him a very modern ring. He perhaps should truly be called ''the father of modern theology'' (or at least ''modernist theology'').[17]

Wilhelm Dilthey (1833-1911), who taught at Berlin at the turn of the century, was also interested in the general theory of human understanding and some of the issues Schleiermacher had raised. He agreed with the concept of the interpreter's shared humanity with the writer and believed in the possibility of entering vicariously into the history or experience of the text and its author. Dilthey's philosophy would, in turn, influence another dominant modern theologian: Rudolf Bultmann (1884-1976).

Bultmann drew upon Dilthey's insights and especially those of another philosopher, Martin Heidegger (1899-1976), who (along with Kierkegaard) largely supplied the existentialist basis to Bultmann's theology. For Bultmann modern science had proven that the universe is a closed causal nexus in which traditional Christian concepts of supernatural revelation through prophecy, miracle, incarnation, resurrection, and the like (and certainly an inspired, authoritative Bible) are simply untenable. The New Testament,

---

[17]See Anthony C. Thiselton, *The Two Horizons* (Grand Rapids MI: William B. Eerdmans Publishers, 1980) 103-107; Richard E. Palmer, *Hermeneutics* (Evanston IL: Northwestern University Press, 1969) 84-97. Thiselton's work may be the most helpful single volume to consult for clarification of the issues in the area of philosophical hermeneutics.

therefore, must be "demythologized" and its message reinterpreted to address modern people's existential questions. Bultmann built upon Heidegger's language analysis, as did some of his disciples who became proponents of the "New Hermeneutic."

Scholars such as Ernst Fuchs and Gerhard Ebeling have continued the Schleiermacher-Dilthey-Heidegger-Bultmann heritage, which turns the task of biblical interpretation into a philosophical language game of sorts that denies that there is a single meaning (along with any other logically implied meanings) for the text which serves as an objective control for contemporary meanings and applications.[18] The value of this school of thought is the insight that the interpreter must be aware of his or her own historical and cultural limitations and remain open to the text so as to allow it to alter the questions and expectations he or she brings to it. This is a valid application of the "hermeneutical circle." The fallacy of the new hermeneutic has been poignantly summarized by D. A. Carson: "It follows, then, that the new hermeneutic pursues 'what is true for me' at the expense of 'what is true.' Theology proper becomes impossible."[19]

EVANGELICAL HERMENEUTICS

It may come as a surprise to many that evangelicals have apparently given a fair hearing to nonevangelical theologians committed to newer hermeneutical methods and sought where possible to apply the valid insights achieved. Anthony Thiselton's *The Two Horizons* is a very sophisticated and sympathetic treatment of the new hermeneutical school of thought. He seems to be in strong agreement with the basic conclusions that in interpreting Scriptures one must both maintain the tension between the past and the present and, at the same time, pursue the goal of the "fusion of horizons" to attain a present-day impact and significance.[20] Thiselton is also able to communicate his hermeneutical insights in a more popular form for believers who are concerned with making practical use of the insights attained by the scholars.[21]

---

[18]Even Thiselton himself has not apparently broken completely free from the subjective enmeshment of the new hermeneutics, at least as far as keeping original meanings intact is concerned. See R. G. Gruenler, "The New Hermeneutic," *Evangelical Dictionary of Theology*, ed. Walter A. Elwell (Grand Rapids MI: Baker Book House, 1984) 765.

[19]Carson, "Hermeneutics," 15. Hans-Georg Gadamer has systematized and expanded this hermeneutical tradition in his important work, *Truth and Method* (New York: Crossroads, 1975).

[20]See for example, Thiselton, *The Two Horizons*, 314-19.

[21]See his "Understanding God's Word Today," in *The Lord Christ*, ed. John Stott, vol. 1 of *Obeying Christ in a Changing World*, ed. John Stott (Cleveland: Collins and World, 1977) 90-122.

J. I. Packer is quicker to point up the deviations and dangers of the newer methods, but he himself is also willing to adapt certain concepts. He shows very skillfully how the so-called "hermeneutical circle" is better understood as a spiral. Within this spiral even the evangelicals' commitment to what they perceive as the Scripture's own teaching concerning the nature of its inspiration and authority can be tested by the interaction between the text and interpreter as described in the new hermeneutic.[22]

D. A. Carson courageously tackles the problem of the relationship between biblical exegesis and systematic theology in the face of the assertion that the diversity of the New Testament teachings makes systematic theology a virtually impossible task. His evaluative response to James D. G. Dunn's *Unity and Diversity in the New Testament,* a volume which definitely puts the accent on diversity, undergirds his analysis of theological methodology. He maintains that there is definitely a linear movement from exegesis to biblical theology (with a reference to historical theology) and then on to systematic theology. However, instead of bending this line into a vicious hermeneutical *circle* which suggests that there are no objective controls, as some theologians have done, Carson argues that the linear model serves as the final control while at the same time there are lines of references back-and-forth among the various disciplines in refining the resultant theological statements. This approach allows the evangelical theologian to work within the guidelines of biblical authority fairly and self-critically.[23]

On the whole, evangelicals seem to be continually refining their views on the authority, inspiration, infallibility, and inerrancy of Scriptures—although at times their dialogues have turned into out-and-out battles! They have also looked very carefully at the newer hermeneutical questions and responded constructively. A very sophisticated evangelical hermeneutical program seems to be emerging.[24] Perhaps brief mention should be made of two newer developments because of their obvious relevance to the topic of this paper.

---

[22]J. I. Packer, "Infallible Scripture and the Role of Hermeneutics," in *Scripture and Truth,* ed. D. A. Carson and John D. Woodbridge (Grand Rapids MI: Zondervan Publishing House, 1983) esp. 348f.

[23]D. A. Carson, "Unity and Diversity in the New Testament: The Possibility of Systematic Theology," in ibid, 65-95, see esp. 91f. See also James D. G. Dunn, *Unity and Diversity in the New Testament: An Inquiry into the Character of Earliest Christianity* (Philadelphia: Westminster Press, 1977).

[24]See the impressive volume published by the International Council on Biblical Inerrancy (ICBI): Earl D. Radmacher and Robert D. Preus, eds., *Hermeneutics, Inerrancy, and the Bible* (Grand Rapids MI: Zondervan, 1984), a compendium of substantive articles and responses on virtually every hermeneutical issue.

The thunderous impact of the "new right" is apparent to all, and evangelicals across the entire theological and political continuum have generally been more vocal and active within society. One less known phenomenon in this ferment is the theonomic movement. R. J. Rushdoony, Greg L. Bahnsen, Gary North, and others have put forward hermeneutical arguments to the effect that God's laws must have direct application in modern society and that officials of the state are responsible to enforce those laws.[25] Their attempts at applying the Christian world view to culture in its totality are commendable, although there have evidently been instances of imbalance and legalism in their positions. John Jefferson Davis seems to be employing the best insights of this movement in his steps toward a comprehensive systematic theology. One can only hope that in the years to come Davis will produce a work (comparable to Erickson's newest effort) which develops the starting position he so skillfully and helpfully lays out in his *Foundations of Evangelical Theology*.[26] Davis has also shown interest in another hermeneutical issue gaining popularity among evangelicals: contextualization.

Perhaps the most significant hermeneutical issue of which some evangelicals have become aware is that of cultural dynamics. Specifically and positively, I am referring to their growing awareness that the pertinence and transforming power of the authoritative teaching of Scripture must be demonstrated within modern society. Both David Wells and John Jefferson Davis of Gordon-Conwell Theological Seminary have issued a clarion call for a contextualized evangelical theology that will transform American society.[27] In addition, evangelicals, perhaps because of their increasing cross-pollination with charismatics, are giving a large role to the Holy Spirit in understanding and applying the Bible's message.

CHARISMATIC HERMENEUTICS

J. I. Packer has noted that evangelicals have too often failed to realize the full significance of the Spirit's role in enabling a believer to understand the Scriptures.[28] They have frequently left the impression that all one needs is a

---

[25]See for example R. J. Rushdoony, *Institutes of Biblical Law* (Nutley NJ: Craig Press, 1973).

[26]John Jefferson Davis, *Foundations of Evangelical Theology* (Grand Rapids MI: Baker Book House, 1984).

[27]See David F. Wells, "An American Evangelical Theology: The Painful Transition from *Theoria* to *Praxis*," in *Evangelicalism in Modern America,* ed. George Marsden (Grand Rapids MI: William B. Eerdmans Publishers, 1984) 83-94; Davis, *Foundations,* 60-72; Davis, ed., *The Necessity of Systematic Theology,* 2nd ed. (Grand Rapids MI: Baker Book House, 1978) 169-90.

[28]Packer, "Infallible Scripture," 347.

mastery of basic principles of interpretation and a keen, creative intellect. Obviously, these qualities are desirable; yet they are woefully inadequate according to the Bible's own testimony.

One of the major strengths of Clark Pinnock's latest effort in the area of biblical authority lies in precisely this area. Pinnock notes the strong rationalism of both liberals and conservatives who neglect the reality and necessity of the Spirit's activity in connection with the Word. They have forgotten that it is the Spirit's role to enable faith and understanding. "If we were to do justice to the Spirit in relation to the Word, I suspect we might get free of some of our cul-de-sacs and find the whole hermeneutical operation loosened up and made exciting."[29]

Packer makes several other important points. First, he reminds us of the Spirit's activity in the five-fold process by which the Scriptures were given to us: revelation, inspiration, canonization, preservation, and translation. Then he discusses the Spirit's witness authenticating the Bible, the Spirit's illumination of our minds, and the Spirit's guidance in the activities of interpretation and application.[30] One wonders whether this growing evangelical awareness of the importance of the Spirit's role could not be attributed in large measure to the astounding impact of the pentecostal/charismatic movement of this century.

As an active participant in charismatic renewal for more than twenty years, I have noted that believers of almost every theological stripe come into a strong confidence in the inspiration and authority of the Bible through their renewal experiences. Furthermore, they often claim that the Scriptures "come alive" to them; they are generally strongly motivated to read them. Dennis Bennett, a pioneering leader in charismatic renewal, shares an interesting personal story in this regard.

Bennett was raised to believe that the Bible is merely a hodgepodge collection of religious literature from which scholars alone could adequately ferret authentic insights. Accepting the entirety of the Scriptures as the work of the Holy Spirit was foreign to him. Yet after receiving the "baptism in the Holy Spirit," Bennett found himself drawn to the Bible and uncomfortable with his former teaching. "It was not an intellectual decision; it was just that I could not be spiritually comfortable taking a patronizing or critical attitude

---

[29]Pinnock, *The Scripture Principle*, 155. Pinnock devotes an entire section of his book to the role of the Holy Spirit. Unfortunately, there are some snakes in Pinnock's garden. One wonders why, for example, he views the story of Peter's getting the coin from the fish's mouth (Matt. 17:24-27) as having "the feel of a legendary feature." Ibid., 125. If one accepts the greatest miracle of all, the resurrection, why should any other reported miracle be troublesome?

[30]J. I. Packer, *Keep in Step with the Spirit* (Old Tappan NJ: Revell, 1984) 239.

toward the Book!''[31] One particular night in a Bible study class, tongues and interpretation came forth in a surprising fashion to solve a very difficult situation. In a dramatic way the words ''This is My Book! I am the Lord!'' chastened the group and gave Bennett a simple but profound formula for expressing a proper attitude toward Scripture.[32]

Could it be that many theologians come to the Scriptures with naturalistic presuppositions simply because they lack a requisite spiritual experience? Biblical phenomena such as miracles, healings, exorcisms, prophecies, tongues, and the like must be ''demythologized,'' in large measure because the interpreter has never had a first-hand encounter with these realities. Pentocostals and charismatics relate naturally to passages about such things, since they have personally experienced many of these supernatural manifestations.

Perhaps the most important contribution the Holy Spirit renewal can make in the area of hermeneutics is a religious one. Through pointing the church back to her very life-breath, through the promotion of spiritual renewal, through reminding the church of the ''God-breathed'' nature of the Bible, and through working signs and wonders, proponents of Holy Spirit renewal may be aiding the church in her quest to understand and apply biblical truth in a fundamental way. Hermeneutical discussion among the theologians has left for too long the impression that the meaning and impact of the Bible can be attained solely through rationalistic and aesthetic abilities. What a blindness that they have failed, literally, to consult the Book's ultimate Author!

FUTURE PROSPECTS

Having said all this, I would be quick to dispel any fears of anti-intellectualism. The answer to ''bad scholarship'' is not ''no scholarship'' but ''good scholarship.'' Even the simplest saints would be deprived of the Scriptures in their native tongues were it not for the scholars who do the translating. Could it not be true that God may ''gift'' some to serve in scholarly capacities? The New Testament lists of *charismata* were never to be taken as exhaustive.

In all probability the hermeneutical explorations in the philosophical areas will continue unabated, and numerous insights will be gleaned. Christians across theological lines will more than likely increase their interaction with each other. Conservative and experiential Christianity seems to be on the ascendency. And perhaps the Puritan divine, John Robinson was right when he said, ''the Lord has more light and truth yet to break forth out of his holy Word.'' We may all have to learn greater humility in relation to the Spirit of

---

[31]Dennis J. Bennett, *Nine O'Clock in the Morning* (Plainfield NJ: Logos, 1970) 88.

[32]Ibid.

God. The everyday saint may come to appreciate sound scholarship more than ever. And the scholar may come to admit with Pinnock that the ''nonexpert in a spirit of receptivity may understand the text better than the expert with all his or her scholarly tools.''[33]

The future belongs to those who ''keep in step with the Spirit'' (Galatians 5:25). Perhaps there is no better way to conclude than with these piercing words from Clark H. Pinnock:

> But if it is true that the presence of the Spirit is essential for the work of interpretation to be effective, then it follows that the practitioners must be believers filled with the Spirit. They must be people who are personally in touch with the reality of God in our midst pointed out so vividly by Saint Luke. They must be those on whom the power has fallen (Luke 24:49), who operate out of radical faith and in the gifts of the Spirit that bear directly upon discerning the will of the Lord. . . . [We] need, in addition to our rational training, a liberation of our spirits by the Spirit of God, so that we might be the kind of interpreters of Scripture that it deserves.[34]

Come, Holy Spirit! We need Thee![35]

---

[33]Pinnock, *The Scripture Principle*, 169.

[34]Ibid., 173f.

[35]In my view, Dale Moody has exemplified this model as few others have done. Almost twenty years ago he wrote: ''Careful scholarship and the charismatic community can be united, and this is a great need of our time.'' Dale Moody, *Spirit of the Living God* (Philadelphia: Westminster Press, 1968) 10. In his voluminous writings and in his enthusiastic teaching and preaching ministry throughout the world he has addressed that need persistently. He is a man of learning and burning—''aglow with the Spirit.'' And I will be eternally grateful for his impact on my life.

THE PROBLEM OF APOSTASY IN NEW TESTAMENT THEOLOGY

I. HOWARD MARSHALL
KING'S COLLEGE
UNIVERSITY OF ABERDEEN
ABERDEEN SCOTLAND

INTRODUCTION

It may seem slightly odd that someone who knows Dale Moody only through the printed word and who has had no particular associations with The Southern Baptist Theological Seminary should take part in this symposium in Dr. Moody's honor, when there are doubtless many others who have a better claim than I. The basis for my invitation to contribute to this volume is that Dr. Moody and I share a common interest in the subject of apostasy and have both written on it. Thus, I have been asked to write on the topic of apostasy and to do so in the light of Dr. Moody's work. I am well aware that the topic can easily raise theological hackles, and I trust that what follows will be taken as an attempt to understand the Word of God in the Scriptures, since they alone can constitute our supreme authority in faith and in practice.

Perhaps an autobiographical word may be helpful as an introduction to the subject. In 1969 I published a book entitled *Kept by the Power of God* with the subtitle *A Study of Perseverance and Falling Away*.[1] The book was

---

[1] I. Howard Marshall, *Kept by the Power of God: A Study of Perseverance and Falling Away* (London: Epworth Press, 1969).

a shortened and somewhat simplified version of a thesis I had completed for the University of Aberdeen six years earlier. I did not find it easy to interest a publisher, a fact which may indicate that, quite apart from the shortcomings of the book in itself, the topic was not one of general concern to the theological public. The publisher for his part may have regretted his rashness in undertaking the assignment; he did not print a lot of copies and not many of them were sold, with the result that the book was withdrawn from circulation after a comparatively short time. Yet it found one "convert." My friend, Professor Clark H. Pinnock, confessed that my book had exercised a decisive influence on his thinking in this area, and as a result of his enthusiasm in exposing the North American evangelical constituency to its arguments the book was republished with some slight revisions in 1975.[2]

The line of thought I developed was not, of course, original. The distinguished scholar whom we are honoring in this volume had come to similar conclusions at an earlier date. He in turn was dependent on the great Baptist scholar, A. T. Robertson. He has developed his position in one of the chapters of his comprehensive study of Christian doctrine, *The Word of Truth*.[3] Another scholar who has also defended the same general position is Robert Shank in his books *Life in the Son*[4] and *Elect in the Son*.[5] A similar position was taken earlier by scholars of the Arminian persuasion, including John Wesley.

The reaction of scholars in the strict Calvinist tradition is to reject the position of writers like Moody and myself. They find the position indefensible on three grounds.

First, they regard the texts in the New Testament which appear to teach the final security of the believer as representing the clear and central teaching of Scripture. They say that other passages which may appear to teach differently, for example, by suggesting the possibility of apostasy, must be interpreted in line with the first texts on the grounds that scriptural teaching by definition is consistent.

Second, the systematic formulation of Christian dogmatics by Calvinist theologians leads to a set of basic and mutually related principles which include the final perseverance of the saints. If one grants that God determined from all eternity to save the elect, then the final perseverance of the elect follows logically. Similarly, if it is agreed that Christ offered an efficacious sac-

---

[2]Ibid., (Minneapolis MN: Bethany Fellowship, 1975).

[3]Dale Moody, *The Word of Truth* (Grand Rapids; William B. Eerdmans Publishing Co., 1981) 348-65.

[4]Robert Shank, *Life in the Son* (Springfield MO: Westcott Publishers, 1961).

[5]Ibid., *Elect in the Son* (Springfield MO: Westcott Publishers, 1970).

rifice and wrought a full salvation for the elect, then it is inconceivable that this salvation does not contain the element of perseverance.

There is a third reason that is also important, although it does not stand on the same level as the other two. This says that the thought is not congenial that I, a believer, may possibly fall away from my faith and my hope of ultimate salvation. Modern sociological study has shown us how much we need a sense of security if we are to cope with life and its problems, and the importance of a secure basis for early life in the caring love of parents has received the stress it deserves. If we need security on the human level, how much more do we need to be able to trust in God to keep us for time and eternity. How important it is that in our Christian life we have the security provided by God, and the knowledge that, whatever we do, nothing can separate us from his love or thwart his purpose for our lives.

Here, then, are three strong reasons for (1) criticizing a position which acknowledges the danger of falling away from the faith, and (2) for arguing that it rests on an unacceptable and false interpretation of Scripture. Some Calvinists will reject the position more or less out of hand. Others, however, recognize a genuine problem of biblical interpretation. Here, special mention must be made of two scholars. The one is Donald A. Carson, whose book, *Divine Sovereignty and Human Responsibility: Biblical Perspectives in Tension*, published in 1981, tackles the problem with particular reference to the Gospel of John and at a profound and scholarly level.[6]. The other is Judy Gundry-Volf, whose dissertation on the problem of perseverance in the writings of Paul, although not yet published, bids fair to be the most detailed and acute study of the topic thus far.[7]

What follows now is an attempt to look again at apostasy from an exegetical point of view using Moody's contribution as a starting point. In the course of the discussion I shall, for sake of convenience, refer to theologians who believe in the final perseverance of the elect as ''Calvinists.'' I shall refer to those who do not accept this doctrine in the way in which it was formulated at Dort[8] as ''non-Calvinists,'' since many of us who are unhappy with Dort are not happy to be lumped together as ''Arminians.''

---

[6]Donald A. Carson, *Divine Sovereignty and Human Responsibility: Biblical Perspectives on Tension* (London: Marshall, Morgan and Scott, 1981).

[7]Judy Gundry-Volf, ''Perseverance and Falling Away in Paul's Thought,'' (Inaugural-Dissertation zur Erlangung des Doktorwürde der Evangelisch-theologischen Fakultät an der Eberhard-Karls-Universität zu Tübingen, 1987).

[8]At the 1618-1619 church synod held at Dort in the Netherlands the doctrines of the Remonstrants (the followers of Jacob Arminius) were condemned in a statement which outlined five key doctrines of Calvinism: the total depravity of mankind; God's unconditional election of those whom he chooses to save; the limitation of the saving efficacy of the atonement to the elect; the irresistibility of God's grace in saving the elect; and the infallible preservation of the

While it is true that an important part of my own upbringing has been in the Methodist Church, I am by no means a "dyed-in-the-wool" Methodist and I owe a great deal to Christians in many other churches. My primary loyalty is to the Word of God written in Scripture and not to any human denomination or theological group. My concern, therefore, is to establish what Scripture actually says, and I am grateful for the impulses from theologians of all camps who open my eyes to see things that otherwise any personal bias might prevent me from seeing. I hope that it is not inappropriate for me to regard it as part of my theological task to help other people to shed their blinders.

SOME MORAL AND PHILOSOPHICAL PROBLEMS

First of all, however, let us mention briefly some of the theological and philosophical problems that the issue raises.

The upholders of the possibility of apostasy are not of course unaware of passages in Scripture which promise that God's people will persevere, but they make the point that these promises are for those who continue to abide in Christ and keep on following the Lord. But the Calvinist will ask whether that is an adequate form of assurance. It is some comfort to know that even if I turn away from the Lord, I can always turn back to him and find him willing to forgive. But knowing how fallible I am, I want the assurance that I can never turn away from the Lord to such an extent that I cannot turn back to him.

And here comes the problem. On the Calvinist view, the possibility of a return means that the Lord himself must so work in my life that I am preserved from the possibility of falling away by his overruling of my sinful will. Thus we find that perseverance depends on a divine determinism that overrules what I myself apparently do in freedom. And so, although the Lord may let me fall into sin, he never lets me sin to such a degree that I become totally deaf to his voice. He overrules my will so that I remain faithful. Indeed, he overruled my will in the first instance, so that I freely turned to him and became a believer.

To be sure, we all believe in the influence of the Holy Spirit in our hearts to transform our stubborn, sinful wills, and we insist that "every thought of holiness, and every victory won are his alone," but this way of looking at things does raise some problems.

---

elect to final salvation. It is the last of these points which is under discussion in this essay, but upholders of Dort would insist that all five points stand or fall together. For a brief account of the Synod see (for example) W. Elwell, ed., *Evangelical Dictionary of Theology* (Grand Rapids: Baker Book House, 1984) 331f.

(1) The Calvinist position cannot explain why it is that the converted sinner still sins some times and to some extent, and why God does not sanctify him entirely at conversion. In effect, God is left deciding to allow the convert to sin on some occasions (but never to the point of apostasy), and at other times to do good.

(2) This means that in the end it is not the preaching or reading of God's Word or any other external means of warning and persuasion that ultimately causes our salvation and holiness, but rather salvation all depends on the secret influence of the Spirit of God on our wills in accordance with a divine plan.

(3) Consequently, the Calvinist view deprives the individual of real will power. When the person does wrong, it is because evil has control of him, rather than God. He is reduced to a mere automaton, apparently free to choose, but in reality at the mercy of the power of evil or the power of good. However, the believer does not know this, and perhaps it does not matter, because he acts as though he were free. The Calvinist can thus insist that divine determinism and human freedom are compatible. However, this view does seem to deny the reality of the personhood of God's creatures. Above all, it does not do justice to those passages in Scripture which clearly show that God treats people as free agents, able to decide for themselves.

(4) The Calvinist position also has serious consequences for the doctrine of God, for it considers the individual's conversion purely an arbitrary act of God. The convert had been a sinner because sin had taken control of him—he had been dead in trespasses and sins from the time of his conception. But God acted to take control of his life and to deliver him from sin. However, no reason can be assigned as to why God chooses some individuals and rejects others (or, if you prefer, passes them by). Thus the problem is that God appears to be capricious in granting his love. He may be steadfast in his love to the elect, but his choice of the elect is arbitrary. Of course, one may reply that God is free to show or to withhold mercy as he chooses, and so he is. But is it just to show mercy only to some? Shall not the judge of all the earth do right?

(5) Finally, there is a philosophical problem in that this view presents God as the prisoner of his own predestining purpose. Were it merely a case of God's determining what other persons do, the problem would not be so great. In fact, however, predestination affects not only what God's creatures do but also what he himself does in relation to them. God decides whether or not he will act to save them. A solution to this problem may be to say that within God purposing and acting occur simultaneously since God is outside time, and therefore the idea that God first purposes and then acts is a mistaken one.

But the determinist view does seem to me to make God the prisoner of his own will.[9]

The effect of these comments is to suggest that in the concept of predestination (whereby everything we do is predetermined) the basis of final perseverance contains moral and logical difficulties and leads to antinomies.

On the other hand, the non-determinist view also has problems. It does not explain how it is that God undoubtedly moves us at times by the working of his Spirit independently of our own wills. Also, it has to come to terms with those passages in Scripture which suggest that salvation from start to finish is the work of God who acts according to his own will. The non-determinist position also shares with the determinist view the problem of explaining the relation of God to evil.

Thus there are problems for both Calvinists and for non-Calvinists. I believe that these difficulties are inherent in any attempt to explain both the actions of God, who is not bound by time and space, and the way in which his actions impinge upon the world he created. Even though we cannot understand in principle how the eternal God functions to cause events in this world, I have the impression that the Calvinist has the greater set of problems. However, I am not philosopher enough to take the matter any further, and therefore I would not want overly to emphasize the fact that I find the greater difficulties in the Calvinist position.

WARNINGS AND ENCOURAGEMENTS TO PERSEVERE

I therefore turn to the area where I feel more at home, namely asking what the New Testament says. A brief review of the textual material discussed by Moody affords a good starting point for this investigation.

In regard to the Gospels Moody is content to appeal to Luke 8:9-15. He is on strong ground in this passage. The interpretation of the Parable of the Sower indicates that there are people who receive the Word but do not persevere or continue in faith. Commentators have seen two ways to apply the lesson of the parable. On the one hand, it may be seen as a warning to its hearers to beware of the temptations to give up believing and to stand firm against them. On the other hand, it may be seen as an explanation for the disciples of what will happen to different groups of people who respond to their mission. Either way we have a clear warning against the danger and therefore the possibility of accepting the Word and falling away.

There are various ways of avoiding this conclusion.

---

[9]For a fuller discussion of some of these points, see C. H. Pinnock, ed., *Grace Unlimited* (Minneapolis: Bethany Fellowship, 1975).

(1) It can be argued that the presence of this and similar warnings in Scripture is part of the means by which God effectually keeps believers from falling away. The purpose of a warning such as this is not to describe actual cases of believers falling away but to describe the fate of hypothetical apostates in such terms that all believers who hear will be persuaded to remain in the faith. In other words, one of the means by which God enables his elect to persevere is through warning them in ways like this.

Now, if one holds that these warnings work in this way, one must also hold that God creates in the elect the correct response to these warnings and that his hidden action in the heart is what leads to perseverance in the end of the day.

But where is the evidence that this is the actual intent of Scriptures such as the present one? And is it not unreal to paint a picture of the fate of hypothetical apostates when such people do not and cannot exist?

(2) It can be argued that the descriptions of people who fall away are in every case descriptions of people who had never in fact believed. They may have accepted the message with joy, but they did not believe. However, this explanation comes to grief on the wording in Luke. The presence of the word "believe" in verse 13 and the contrast with verse 12 indicate that these are people who believe for a time. It is necessary, therefore, to claim that a distinction may be drawn between real and temporary or half-hearted belief. Or the distinction is between those who merely believe on a human level and those in whose hearts the Spirit kindles true belief. However it be expressed, this interpretation would be that such passages as the present one do not describe the elect but rather those whose faith was never of the saving variety.

Of these alternatives the second would appear to be the easier to defend. But let us note clearly what is happening. What this exegesis amounts to is that Luke teaches that a person will not be saved unless his faith is marked, positively, by holding fast the Word, bearing fruit and demonstrating endurance, and, negatively, by not ceasing to believe in times of temptation or by not yielding to temptations. In other words, the parable is about the attitudes that believers must show: they are commanded to persevere, and they are told that, if they do not, they will be lost, just like those people who never believed at all. Thus, in the end of the day it will be seen that they did not have saving faith, since their faith did not last and was not strong enough to overcome temptation. It would appear, however, that up to that point they did believe.

The parable says that saving faith is persevering faith. But this surely carries the implication that at any given moment it is impossible to say of a person that he has saving faith; the only proof of saving faith is that the person persevered in the faith and died believing. (We can ignore the problem of people who died at a point when it was not possible for them any longer to demonstrate conscious faith. No one is going to deny salvation to such people.)

If we put the point in this way, we have stated precisely what the defender of the possibility of apostasy is stating. For the parable does not teach that people will infallibly persevere in faith; it simply describes the fact that there are people who do. Certainly I cannot look at my faith at this moment and say, "Yes, so far my faith has lasted, withstood temptation and brought forth fruit, and therefore I can be confident of my future salvation," for I do not know what tomorrow will bring—at least so far as this parable is concerned.

The Calvinist interpreter, then, is saying: people who do not bring forth fruit and persevere show that they were not of the elect and that they never had saving faith. A typical presentation of the position is: "Men must hold themselves responsible to persevere; but if they do so, it is God's grace upholding them; while if they fall away, *they demonstrate that they were not true disciples in the first place.*"[10] The non-Calvinist says: if people wish to attain to final salvation, they must persevere in faith, and only at the end will it be seen whether they persevered. For the Calvinist there is a quality in the initial faith which guarantees perseverance (or, God who inspired the faith will enable it to persevere), so that we can say that such a person was and is "a true disciple." The non-Calvinist, while not disputing that one can distinguish broadly between nominal and true believers, insists that perseverance is not so much a quality inherent in true faith at the point of conversion, as it is simply the lastingness of faith that is shown from moment to moment throughout the Christian life.

Thus one can read the parable from a Calvinist perspective. But one must insist: (a) that this perspective is not necessary for understanding the parable in itself; (b) that the parable (and similar teaching) does not *prove* the Calvinist interpretation.

Hence such a parable as this does not *teach* final perseverance. To the Calvinist and the non-Calvinist believer alike it says: see that you persevere! Of itself it does not convey to the believer the assurance that he will persevere. We shall find that this is true for the "warning" passages in general.

Moody briefly notes two passages in Acts which favor his position. One is the Ananias and Sapphira story (Acts 5:1-11). However, I do not think that any conclusions regarding the ultimate fate of the two sinners can be drawn from this passage. The Acts 20:30 text is a warning to the church that fierce wolves will draw disciples away after them. Again, the Calvinist may claim that those who are drawn away were not "true" disciples, but in order to do so it is necessary to demonstrate that Luke (or Paul) distinguishes between true and seeming disciples.

---

[10]Carson, *Divine Sovereignty and Human Responsibility, 195;* italics are mine.

If the latter are meant, then (on Calvinist premises) the warning would appear to be futile because the seeming disciples do not belong to the elect. If it be argued that the purpose of the warning is to help any of these seeming disciples who are elect but not yet regenerate to come to true faith, then it must be remarked that this is a peculiar form of wording for the purpose. If the former group is meant, then the passage is being interpreted on the hypothesis that those who persevere to the end and do not become the prey of wolves are in fact the elect, and that they persevered because they were predestined to do so.

But does this really help? The fact is that no one can know for certain who are the true disciples and the false disciples. If a person is in the former group, he has still to heed the warning: only by so doing can he show that he is one of the elect. In other words, the Calvinist "believer" cannot fall away from "true" faith, but he can "fall away" from what proves in the end to be only seeming faith. The possibility of falling away remains. But in neither case does the person know for certain whether he is a true or a seeming disciple. All that he knows is that Christ alone can save and that he must trust in Christ, and that he sees signs in his life which may give him some assurance that he is a true disciple. But these signs may be misleading.

It comes down to a question of assurance. Whoever said, "The Calvinist knows that he cannot fall from salvation but does not know whether he has got it," had it summed up nicely. On this view the ground of assurance is the evidence of a changed life. But this can be counterfeit and misleading. The non-Calvinist knows that he has salvation—because he trusts in the promises of God—but is aware that, left to himself, he could lose it. So he holds fast to Christ. It seems to me that the practical effect is the same.

Moody then turns to the epistles of Paul. Here he notes the encouragements and warnings to Christians and the fear that some would fall. The issues here are in principle the same as in the passages already discussed. And in a sense the exegetes are in agreement. For the Calvinist the warnings and the promises are the means by which God urges the elect to faithfulness on the empirical, human level, while he works in their hearts so that they respond positively. For the non-Calvinist the same passages are equally God's means of urging believers to persevere. In both cases it is recognised that the Spirit is the means of renewal without which believers would be unable to respond to God's word. The question is whether the Spirit always operates irresistibly and positively in the lives of some but not of others. Whether I am a Calvinist or not, I must heed the encouragements and warnings, in the former case to show that I am a real and not a seeming believer, and in the latter case for fear that I might fall away from the real faith that I have.

Most important are the passages in Hebrews to which Moody gives special attention. There are five of these: 2:1-4 (we must pay close attention to what we have heard, lest we drift from it); 3:7-4:13 (the danger of having an evil, unbelieving heart and thus falling away from the living God); 6:1-20 (the impossibility of restoring to repentance those who become partakers of the Holy Spirit and then commit apostasy); 10:19-39 (the punishment in store for those who sin willfully after having been sanctified by the blood of the covenant); and 12:1-29 (the warning not to be like Esau who was given no opportunity to repent after he sold his birthright). The first and second passages can be understood by Calvinists like the cases of seeming believers above, but this is not the most natural interpretation of them. The third passage (Hebrews 6:1-20) causes problems for the Calvinist because it is extremely implausible to interpret the passage as referring to people who were never genuine believers and then claim that the text describes a merely hypothetical danger. The same is true of the fourth passage, and (less clearly) of the fifth. That is to say, the view that the Hebrews passages speak of merely nominal believers is most unlikely. The Calvinist interpretation has to be that the dangers are purely hypothetical, since, it is claimed, God uses the passages effectively to warn all true believers against the danger of apostasy. But the passages in themselves do not require this interpretation, and it is safe to say that it would never have been offered except in the interests of a dogmatic theory that God will infallibly save a fixed group of the elect. However, even though the author of Hebrews emphasizes the faithfulness of God to his people, there is no suggestion in the text that the author shares this particular view of predestination.

ELECTION AND PRESERVATION

We now have on the one hand, a series of statements apparently addressed to believers, urging perseverance, warning against apostasy, and indicating the unpleasant consequences of apostasy. The believer must take these warnings seriously. But he is encouraged to persevere by the promises of the help of the Spirit of God, the fatherly love of God, and by other gracious inducements.

On the other hand, as Moody recognizes, there is another strand of teaching which speaks of God's election of his people and of his will to bring them to final salvation. This is found especially in the Gospel of John where we have the statements of Jesus that his sheep will never perish. Moody discusses John 3:3-8 (those who have been born again cannot be "unborn"); 5:24 (believers pass from death to life and do not come to judgment); 6:37 (all whom the Father gives to the Son will come to him); 6:39 (this is the will of God, that Christ should lose none of those given to him but raise them up at the last day); and especially 10:28 (my sheep shall never perish, and no one shall snatch them out of my hand).

Our problem is the relation between these statements and the former set. There can be only three solutions. The first is to give the election texts the primacy and to reinterpret the warnings to fit in with them by any of the means already discussed. This gives an unnatural rendering to the warnings. The second possibility is to recognize that there is a tension in the passages and not try to avoid it by twisting either set of statements. There is, of course, a third solution which is to give primacy to the warnings and to twist the election statements to mean less than they apparently say. This is probably the least satisfactory solution.

So the question is what we make of the election and preservation sayings. I begin with a comment on the Johannine material. The John 10:28 text says that there is a group of people who are the sheep of the Good Shepherd. Whoever does not belong to this group does not believe. What leads to belief is not seeing signs that prove that Jesus is the Messiah but hearing (that is, obeying) his voice and following him. Those who believe have eternal life and no one can take them out of the Shepherd's care—not even the Evil One. The reason no one can do this is that the Father who gave the flock to Jesus is greater than any other power.

It is surely one thing for the Devil to snatch the sheep away against the sheep's will—that cannot happen. It is another thing for the sheep to yield to temptation. How, then, is the activity of the Devil seen? Does he merely tempt or does he cause people to fall? Is his appeal irresistible? It would be easy if we could say that he merely tempts and that it depends on us whether we fall.

Now on the level of exhortation and teaching, do we tell people that the Devil is irresistible to Christians? Paradoxically, we do tell non-believers that they cannot avoid yielding to temptation, but since they are responsible they should not do so. The Christian schoolteacher does not tell his pupils that they cannot avoid doing what is wrong and that therefore he will not punish them if they commit wrong. Or do we tell people that the Spirit is irresistible, and that they can sit back and let the Spirit take control? Some may do so, but this attitude of "quietism" would probably be rejected by serious theologians. What we actually do is to tell believers to resist the Devil in the strength of God. They can win, but they will not win if they do not fight! Thus, whatever we believe about John 10:28, in practice we tell believers that they must resist the Devil, or else they will fall.

Next, we can consider the concept of election. The words "election" and "elect," like the concept, are used in a number of theologically relevant ways: (1) to refer to Jesus as the Chosen One of God; (2) in the plural ("elect") to refer to the church and its members collectively. The second is the most characteristic use. (3) "Election" also refers to the calling of individuals to special tasks such as apostleship (Acts 1:24; 9:15). (4) In the singular, the term "elect" refers to an individual Christian. There seems to be only one possible case of the last usage, namely in reference to Rufus in Romans 16:13. The fact that Rufus is singled out in this way suggests that the word is used here in an unusual manner, perhaps to mean "outstanding" or something similar.

It is important to note that "elect" is always used of those who actually belong to the church, not of prospective believers. The one possible exception is in 2 Timothy 2:10, but there the expression means that Paul labors for the sake of believers so that they will attain to final salvation.

Next, we note that the term is ordinarily used to describe those who belong to the church in terms of outward profession, rather than to distinguish between those who really belong and those who are merely professors. Thus the term is not used of a group within the church secretly known to God. There is a possible exception in Matthew 22:14, but this verse simply refers to those who are invited to the wedding, some of whom are found unworthy; many are called, but only some of them respond and become part of the "elect."

Where then is the source of the idea of a secret group of elect individuals previously chosen by God to be saved and to persevere in salvation? This idea does not come from the use of the term "elect" but from other passages which may suggest that God has chosen some and passed by others. It is of course true that God chooses specific individuals for particular tasks—there is an element of particularity here that cannot be avoided. But are there authentic grounds for extrapolating from the principle of the calling of some individuals to service the conclusion that there is a predestination of those who are called to salvation? And does it in any case follow that those called to service will necessarily obey? Judas fell away from being one of the Twelve, and Paul gives the impression that he responded of his own choice (Acts 26:19). But it must be said that for a Calvinist the fact that somebody is said to respond to grace freely is no argument against effectual calling.

In John 6:64 Jesus states that there are some disciples who do not believe, for (says John) Jesus knew from the beginning who were the unbelievers and the betrayer. But there is nothing particularly problematic here: Jesus knows the hearts of people. Jesus goes on to say that no one can come to him unless it is given to him by the Father. He rejects the idea that people can "control" him. Only if the Father calls can people come. But this does not necessarily mean that if a person is called he will respond with faith.

2 Timothy 2:19 has also been cited in this connection (The Lord knew those who were his people. But this text is only a recognition that the visible church can contain plausible hypocrites who do not really belong to it, and no one denies that this can be the case.

More importance attaches to Romans 8:28-30. These verses say that the people who love God need not be afraid of tribulations (8:18) because the glory in store for them is greater than the tribulation; we can be confident that, no matter what painful experiences we have, all will be for the good of those whom God has called, because his final purpose for those whom he calls is their glorification. We know that because of two things. First, God's purpose for those whom he "foreknew" was that they might share the image of Jesus, that is, share in his glory. Second, God has already started the process: God has called the people for whom he has this purpose. Calling was followed by justification, obviously of those who believed and thereby responded to the call. And justification is followed by a glorification that has already begun (2 Corinthians 3:18). Thus this passage is meant to reassure God's people that his final purpose for them is glorification, a purpose that will be carried out despite their sufferings. The passage is not a statement about the effectual calling of those whom God foreknew. It is a guarantee that those who have responded to God's call with love (and faith) can be fully assured of his purpose of final glorification for them.

Finally, there is a group of texts in Acts which point to election. In Acts 13:48 we find that when Paul preached in Antioch of Pisidia the Gentiles who heard rejoiced and all who were "ordained" to eternal life believed. In 16:14 the Lord opened Lydia's heart to attend to what Paul said. And in 18:10 the Lord assured Paul that he had many people in Corinth, that is, many people who apparently were to be converted. These verses appear to suggest a divine plan to be carried out by Paul involving the salvation of individuals. With regard to Acts 16:14, however, no one would deny that people can hear and respond to the gospel only if the Lord takes the initiative. Acts 18:10 indicates the Lord's foreknowledge of the progress of the gospel in Corinth. But the text could also mean that, since there were now many Christians in Corinth, God's purpose for Paul was that he should continue there to teach them and ground them in the faith. Acts 13:48 could well mean that those Gentiles who had already begun to search for eternal life (like Cornelius in Acts 10) believed upon hearing the good news that salvation was now at last being offered to them through Jesus. Or it might mean that the Gentiles believed inasmuch as they had (collectively) been included in God's saving plan.

We have no desire to empty these verses of their meaning. It is beyond cavil that the Bible teaches that God takes the initiative in salvation, that he planned the creation of his people from eternity past, that it is he who calls to salvation, and that his Spirit leads people to faith in a way that we cannot understand. Calvinist and non-Calvinist alike believe that it makes sense to pray that the Spirit will lead unconverted people to respond. But whether we can conclude from this that a secret predestining will of God always operates when people are saved is doubtful.

Nor is there any question whatever that the Bible clearly teaches the loving purpose of God who keeps believers by his grace (1 Peter 1:5). As Christians we can and do rely completely on Christ, the Good Shepherd, and we claim his promise that he will keep us and that he will not let us fall (Jude

24). We could not live the Christian life without these promises and their gracious realization in our lives.

It is this element of promise that needs to be emphasized to balance Moody's emphasis on the possibility of apostasy; Moody has deliberately offered a one-sided position in order to counterbalance a bias in the opposite direction that misinterprets important parts of Scripture.

CONCLUSION

It is time to conclude. In this essay I have argued:

(1) The New Testament contains encouragements to believers to persevere and warnings against the dangers of apostasy. These warnings are best understood as calls to believers to persevere in the faith in view of genuine dangers. They are not to be understood as calls which "true" believers will inevitably heed because God has predetermined that they shall do so. Warnings in that case would be empty threats, since no one will ever apostatize if predetermined otherwise. Nor should these be understood as warnings addressed to people who are not true believers. Again these would be unreal warnings, since such people would need to be told to repent and believe, rather than told not to turn away from a faith they do not even have.

(2) The New Testament also teaches that God takes the initiative in salvation and leads people to faith by the work of the Spirit. Those who respond to the Gospel become God's people, his "elect." But it is not clear that the New Testament teaches that God has predestined a limited group of people to salvation, and that he effectually calls them and does not effectually call other people.

(3) The New Testament also teaches that God gives his grace and power to his people to enable them to persevere, and that with divine help there is no reason why they should ever fall away from him. Yet the possibility of falling away cannot be excluded. We do not know whether any will in fact fall away and be lost eternally, although there are some possible cases in the New Testament.

(4) It is better not to think of a group of people who at their conversion become "true" believers because of God's election and call and whose faith will therefore inevitably persevere. In fact, on the Calvinist view, no one can ever know for certain that he is one of the elect, and he must constantly seek to make his calling and election sure. Rather, we must say that the New Testament calls on all who believe in Jesus Christ to persevere in belief, that is, to keep on believing. Those who know that they are God's children and have the assurance that their sins are forgiven must go on believing and committing themselves to the saving and keeping love of Jesus. Their assurance of

final salvation does not rest primarily upon the evidence of election but rather on their Savior, and they know that the grace which has been openly revealed in Christ is not cancelled by a secret plan of God which may have excluded them from salvation, even though they have experienced some taste of it.

(5) It emerges that in practice the Calvinist believer is in no better position than the non-Calvinist. According to L. Berkhof[11] there is some difference of opinion among Calvinists as to whether faith includes assurance. Berkhof himself allows that true faith "carries with it a sense of security, which may vary in degree" and that believers can attain to a subjective assurance from contemplating their own experience of the work of the Spirit. But, while many believers in the Calvinist tradition undoubtedly do have assurance of salvation, both present and final (for mercifully God's gifts are not bound by what our theological systems allow him to grant), it is difficult to avoid the impression that a strict Calvinist can never be fully certain that he is one of the elect. As soon as he believes that he is one of the elect, he knows that he cannot fall from grace; but then might he not begin to trifle with sin, and thereby prove he never was elect? The non-Calvinist may believe that there is a danger of his apostasy, but he also believes in the revealed grace of God, and he knows that there is no secret plan of God which may conflict with his revealed will; on the contrary, he knows that he is included in the will of God to "bring many sons to glory," and consequently he knows that he can trust in God with complete confidence.

(6) On both views the possibility of apostasy exists at the experiential level. The Calvinist view allows that people may be seeming believers who in the end will not be saved; they will not persevere in faith because they never had the "real" faith which contains the virtue of perseverance. The non-Calvinist view also allows that people may believe and yet fall away because they did not persevere. But whereas the former view attributed "apostasy" to the fact that God did not elect these people to salvation, the latter view attributes it to the mystery of evil. It can be protested that neither solution is wholly satisfying. The former must allow that God does not show mercy to all, thereby suggesting that he acts immorally. The latter has to allow that, although God acts morally, for some mysterious reason he cannot always conquer the evil in human hearts; but the reason for this lies not in the reprobating will of God but in the mystery of evil. Perhaps, then, in the end it makes little practical difference whether we speak of the mystery of the divine will or of the mystery of evil. But on the theological level there is a serious difference. In both cases we face the problem of evil and admit that we cannot solve it. The former solution is problematic, because it questions the goodness of God and

---

[11]*Systematic Theology* (London: The Banner of Truth Trust, 1969) 507-509.

has to read into much of the New Testament a "hidden agenda" in the divine plan for salvation. The latter solution is also problematic because it appears to question the absolute power of God,[12] but it has perhaps fewer exegetical difficulties, since it does not require us to give an artificial interpretation of such passages as those cited from Hebrews above.

Thus we find that both Calvinists and non-Calvinists affirm the reality of God's preserving grace and both allow for the possibility of apostasy in the church. But an exegetical study of the New Testament makes it quite clear that in view of the complexity of the evidence and the impossibility of denying the reality of the danger of apostasy we are best advised to admit that there is a tension in Scripture on this subject. In the last analysis this tension is due to the impossibility of explaining both the mystery of divine causation and the mystery of evil. Therefore, we should recognize that the strict Calvinist approach offers an oversimplification and systematization of the biblical material. It is to the credit of Dr. Moody that he has expressed his unease with over-systematization of biblical theology and is content to live with mystery.

---

[12]For a helpful discussion of the philosophical problem see J. L. Walls, "Can God save anyone he wills?" *Scottish Journal of Theology* 38 (1985): 155-72.

DALE MOODY'S ECCLESIOLOGY

WAYNE WARD
THE SOUTHERN BAPTIST THEOLOGICAL SEMINARY
LOUISVILLE KY 40208

Most people who have followed the theological writing and teaching of Dale Moody would probably suggest that his primary interest has been the doctrine of salvation. There is no doubt that he has made a significant reinterpretation of the doctrine through his emphasis on salvation as a process, a view he has based on the biblical writers' use of the past, present, and future tenses, all three, in their texts on salvation.[1] Much of his writing and lecturing in recent years has been devoted to this theme, with special attention given to the biblical warnings against apostasy. However, at the beginning of his teaching career during and following World War II, the doctrine of the church was in the center of theological discussion; and Moody plunged into the debate with his characteristic vigor.

HISTORICAL BACKGROUND

In the 1940s and 1950s the doctrine of the church took center stage for a number of reasons. The World Council of Churches had just been formed and it offered hope of reconciliation in a fragmented and divided world. The study

---

[1]The best summary of Moody's doctrine of salvation is found in his systematic theology, *The Word of Truth* (Grand Rapids: William B. Eerdmans Publishing Company, 1981) 308-65. This work is also our primary source for exploring his doctrine of the church.

commissions of the Council brought together scholars of many backgrounds to work on new approaches to the interpretation of Scripture, critical reviews of church traditions, and exploration of common ground among the various communions. The historic main-line churches from the Protestant Reformation were especially enriched and challenged by the inclusion of the Eastern Orthodox tradition in the Council. Even though the gaping omission of Roman Catholics seriously limited the Council's ecumenical discussions, the Orthodox contribution was significant, because it forced the Protestant scholars to confront the claims of hierarchy and succession in a profound way. The exclusiveness of these claims tempered the runaway optimism that sometimes welled up in the early days of the ecumenical movement.

Karl Barth had challenged the World Council to find its basis for unity in the Holy Scriptures.[2] After all, with minor variations, the churches had a common canon of Scripture which offered a specific source for their unity of doctrine and practice. If, as many believed, the new methods of biblical interpretation could bring widespread agreement on the most fundamental doctrines of the faith, there might be some hope of bringing various church traditions together.

The early years of the World Council were exciting times with study of the authority of Scripture, debate and celebration of Holy Communion, and even discussion of topics as controversial as believers' baptism and the apostolic succession of the priesthood. Although the optimism of the decades of the 1940s and 1950s spawned a few mergers of churches—churches which were already very close in their history and doctrine—the study commissions were constantly coming up against a stubborn and painful fact: most of the churchmen were more concerned to justify and defend their church traditions, even when they had to twist or ignore the biblical teachings, than they were to reform their church traditions in the light of the plain teachings of Scripture.

No one fought this battle more ardently than Dale Moody. For years he served as a member of the Faith and Order Commission of the World Council of Churches, and he demonstrated his submission to the authority of Scripture by expanding and correcting his own Baptist tradition at a number of points. Although the congregational understanding of the nature of the church had been bedrock Baptist doctrine through the centuries, Moody found in the Pastoral Epistles support for other patterns of church organization, namely, episcopal and presbyterian. Even the role of the metropolitan bishop, such as

---

[2]This challenge was issued in Barth's address to the Amsterdam Assembly of the World Council of Churches. See "The Church—the Living Congregation of the Living Lord Jesus Christ," in *Man's Disorder and God's Design: the Amsterdam Assembly Series* (New York: Harper & Brothers, n.d.).

Timothy in Ephesus, would suggest a need for Baptists to modify their historic aversion to bishops.

Not only Dale Moody, but many other earnest scholars, were disappointed by the failure of the World Council to break through the entrenched bastions of ministerial power and church traditions. It became evident in the 1960s that there was no hope of reforming the various traditions by a return to the biblical basis for evaluating those traditions. In this situation, two alternatives began to appear. Various voices could be heard on both sides, with several adaptations in between.

One alternative was to emphasize the spiritual unity already present as the gift of the One Lord through the One Spirit. Communion services had already brought to the participants an overwhelming experience of the unity of all true believers in Christ. Even members of those churches who could not cross their doctrinal barriers to experience intercommunion at the Lord's Table were profoundly moved by times of common worship and prayer. The Holy Spirit bore witness to their unity in ways which transcended all their doctrinal differences. Because Moody is a very charismatic Christian, devoted to living and celebrating the work of the Holy Spirit in our lives, he found this dimension of ecumenical Christian experience very appealing. But, like many other scholars, he could not be content with a docetic disembodiment of the church. He felt there ought to be a visible embodiment of this spiritual unity in a church structure and ministry which could express it.

This second alternative was shipwrecked on the shoal of "super-church" fears. Many scholars believed that it might be possible to achieve a broad structure of organic union which at the same time might permit wide diversity of traditions in the practice of evangelism, baptism, the Lord's Supper, and Christian ministry. The ecumenical spirit of Pope John XXIII and the wide-ranging discussions in the Second Vatican Council gave some encouragement to this longing for one truly catholic or universal church which could coordinate the mission and witness of Christ in an increasingly hostile world.

But many feared that this would be an authoritarian super-church that would stifle freedom, punish diversity, and crush dissent, and they blocked any major effort toward the formation of One World Church. Even when the Roman Catholic Communion, under Pope John XXIII, moved toward the World Council with overtures which had not been imagined since the Reformation, many in the Council found themselves ambivalent in their responses. They were thrilled by the Catholic acceptance of them as brethren in Christ and shared some religious exercises with their Catholic brethren and sisters, but they still wondered if their status as "separated brethren" could be overcome only by coming back under the authority of Mother Rome, or the Holy Father.

The political and social tensions of the decades of the 1960s and 1970s changed the agenda of the meetings of the World Council of Churches. Political issues, especially between East and West, and in relation to Third World countries, came to the center of discussion. This is essentially where the ecumenical movement is at the present time. Efforts to find common ground on major doctrines have been replaced by pronouncements on revolutionary movements and support of political and social causes.

It is against this background, especially the period immediately following World War II, that Moody's doctrine of the church must be understood. It still stands as one of the best proposals for finding the unity for which Christ prayed: that we might be one as He and the Father are One.

THEOLOGICAL PRESUPPOSITIONS

In order to give a brief exposition and evaluation of Moody's ecclesiology, it is necessary to keep in mind two or three important presuppositions.

The fundamental presupposition is the authority of Holy Scripture. All doctrine, according to Moody, must be rooted in Holy Scripture, and the doctrine of the church is no exception. Every tradition, including his own, should be evaluated, criticized, and reformed in the light of biblical teaching.

Even though there would be differences of scriptural interpretation, Moody was convinced that there would be far more unanimity in sound biblical scholarship than there is in church creeds. If church authorities were willing to follow the lead of biblical scholars, a great measure of common ground could be found in matters of church doctrine and practice. The truth of this is demonstrated over and over again when biblical scholars of widely differing communions find themselves in agreement on fundamental interpretations of Scripture. At the Ecumenical Institute in Bossey, Switzerland and at Tantur in Jerusalem, I have often found myself in closer agreement with Roman Catholic scholars who are seriously exploring the biblical teachings than I am with Protestant scholars who sometimes take them lightly.

This is still one of our best hopes. Reform comes slowly and painfully; but the constant study of God's Word can set in motion forces, powered by the Holy Spirit, that can eventually bring important changes. The Protestant Reformation is proof of this, and the changes introduced in Roman Catholicism by Vatican II are a modest demonstration of this in our own time. Changing social conditions and exciting insights from Holy Scripture still combine to create new approaches to church doctrine and practice. The failure of biblical study to bring about the complete transformation of our creeds and traditions should not cause us to despair. It is still one of our best hopes for significant change and church renewal.

A second of Moody's assumptions is the dynamic presence and power of the Holy Spirit. Because he is a genuinely charismatic Christian, Moody is one of the most ecumenical persons who has ever walked upon this planet. Born and bred in the Texas Baptist tradition, holding deeply cherished convictions, he is never reluctant to give to anyone a reason for the hope that is in him. Yet, at the same time, he has found a deep and profound spiritual kinship with fellow believers in Roman Catholic, Anglican, Eastern Orthodox, Protestant, and Pentecostal communions. Whether he is worshipping at Roman Catholic Maria Laach in German or leading the eucharistic service at the Ecumenical Institute in Jerusalem, Moody truly revels in the spiritual community which is formed by the Holy Spirit.

It would be impossible to grasp the dynamic view of the church in Moody's theology without recognizing this dominant role of the Holy Spirit in making all believers one body in Christ. Because this unity is the gift of God and is achieved in some measure through and around our differences, it follows that our primary responsibility is to remove the barriers which hinder the working of the Spirit in our individual lives and in our churches and to find positive ways of expressing this unity in the structure, ministry, worship, and mission of the One Church of our Lord Jesus Christ.

A third presupposition of Moody is that we do not need to achieve a rigid uniformity in doctrine or practice. We can live happily with a great deal of diversity in church structure, ministry, and forms of worship. For Moody, it is not a matter of tolerating differences—he can positively rejoice in them, believing that the diversity of traditions enriches the body of Christ.

This glad acceptance of diversity is rooted partly in his conviction that multiple patterns are found, at least incipiently, in the New Testament. Whatever Moody finds in his understanding of the Scriptures, he is prepared to follow all the way. He has done this repeatedly, at great personal cost, even when such a course challenges the most sacred denominational traditions.

Although I have never heard him express this or seen it in his writings, I believe there is another reason for Moody's easy acceptance of diversity in Christian worship, ministry, and polity: he has a profound conviction of the sinfulness of humankind and of the inability of any of us to achieve the perfection for which we long. In such a world all expressions of the church, worship, and ministry will be partial and imperfect. God can use limited and imperfect human vessels; it is all he has to use! Moody can accept radically diverse traditions because he has experienced them and has found the witness of the Spirit even in traditions which differ the most from his own.

A fourth, and last, presupposition should claim our attention. In a way it is the "flip side" of the last one. While Moody can live with diverse expressions of church, ministry, and mission, he would find it exceedingly difficult to live in a tradition which would not allow him the freedom of dissent. In this regard, he is a committed Baptist in the historic tradition of the dissenters.

The priesthood of all believers does involve our ministry to one another in prayer, confession, counsel, and encouragement. But, in our Baptist tradition, it has especially meant our direct access to God without human priest or mediator and the direct Lordship of Christ over congregation and believer without the need of a vicar to represent an absentee Lord. E. Y. Mullins called this "soul competency," competent, that is, to deal directly with God and be accountable directly to God. It is a precious treasure in the Baptist tradition, and it shines throughout Moody's exposition of the doctrine of the church.

SYSTEMATIC EXPOSITION OF THE DOCTRINE

One might summarize almost all that Moody says about the church under the phrase "body of Christ." But he chooses to start his systematic treatment and to ground his entire ecclesiology in the concept of *mission*. Beginning with the *qahal,* the assembly of Israel, and going on to the *ekklesia* as the people of God in the New Covenant, Moody defines the church as mission: "Indeed, the church is mission, and where there is no mission there is no church." God has certainly called the church "out of the world," but He has sent her "back into the world with a message and a mission."

The Mission of the Church

After a brief survey of the mission and message of Jesus in the "five books of Matthew," the only Gospel which uses the word "church," Moody summarizes the mission of the New Testament church in a threefold way: "as *martyria* (witness), *diakonia* (service), and *koinonia* (fellowship)."[3] Anyone who has ever been a student of Dale Moody will recognize in this outline a typical Moodyism. He has a fondness for verbal sequence, alliteration, and logical connection. He has sometimes been criticized for imposing neat patterns upon biblical or historical material thereby finding coherent themes which are not as obvious to others. This may be a characteristic of systematic theologians, who are, after all, trying to find coherence and relationship in a vast body of material. But Moody has a gift approaching genius in his ability to assimilate a great amount of material and organize it in neat and unforgettable categories. Thousands of students who have been stimulated and challenged by his teaching can testify to the effectiveness of this teaching method. It is brilliantly demonstrated in this example on the mission of the church.

The three New Testament terms for the church's mission do not begin with the same letter, but they do have the same ending. More importantly,

---

[3]Moody, *Word of Truth,* 428.

Moody demonstrates that they represent three different emphases in three different traditions in the New Testament.

Martyria (Witness) is the Petrine tradition, found in the three major sources for the Petrine teachings, Acts 1-2, 1 Peter and the Gospel of Mark. Anticipating the criticism that this is one-sided, neglecting other emphases, Moody writes: "This does not mean the Petrine tradition is unconcerned with service and fellowship, but witness is primary." With relentless precision Moody follows this term and the witnessing activity through the Petrine material: Jesus promised his disciples that the Holy Spirit would come upon them and they would be His witnesses (Acts 1:8); Peter voiced the requirement that an apostle to replace Judas must "become with us a witness" to the resurrection of Jesus (Acts 1:22); in his great witnessing sermon at Pentecost Peter proclaimed the resurrection of Jesus and said, "Of that we all are witnesses" (Acts 2:32); he used the same words on Solomon's Porch (Acts 3:15); and, before the Sanhedrin, he added the witness of the Holy Spirit to the witness of the disciples (Acts 5:32).

Moody traces this theme throughout Acts and 1 Peter, climaxing with Peter's portrayal of himself in 1 Peter 5:1, "as a fellow elder and a witness of the sufferings of Christ." Even though Mark does not use the word "witness," Moody finds the whole Gospel to be "a witness to the belief that Jesus was in his death the suffering Servant," with the first half of the Gospel disclosing "the secret of the Son of God (1:1-8:26)" and the second part identifying Jesus "as the Son of God and Son of Man with the suffering Servant (8:27-16:7)."[4]

In a parallel way, Moody follows the theme of *diakonia* (service) through the Pauline tradition and the theme of *koinonia* (fellowship) through the Johannine tradition. Whether one agrees with Moody's characterization of these three traditions under these three Greek terms or not, one fact is indisputable: he has defined and enriched his understanding of the church as mission by exploring in great detail three of the most important traditions in the New Testament. The only effective criticism of this approach would be a demonstration of an even more comprehensive way of bringing the New Testament witness to bear upon the mission of the church today. If that can be done, no one will rejoice more than Dale Moody. That is what he has given his life to, with a vigorous dedication.

It must be remembered that in such a classification of the New Testament traditions, Moody is not offering a cafeteria selection in which one may choose witness, or service, or fellowship. He is saying just the opposite. The church must express all of these, and more, drawing on all the expressions of the

---

[4]*Word of Truth,* 430.

biblical tradition in order to be the church that Christ wants it to be. Because of the limitations which we have as human beings, even as we noted in the section above on "presuppositions," most Christian believers and most Christian churches will not achieve the full and balanced perspective which Moody has outlined. We tend to emphasize certain distinctive practices in each of our denominations. This has been the story of church history. But the value of such an exposition of the varied New Testament traditions is obvious: it gives us an opportunity to reflect upon, correct, and renew our own tradition in the light of the richness of the biblical teachings. This is the way Moody uses the Scriptures in relation to the doctrine of the church or any other doctrine.

The Structures of the Church

Moody is as much at home in historical theology as he is in the Scriptures. He has loved them, read them and taught them for many years. Surprisingly, to those who know him primarily as a biblical theologian, he develops the entire section on structures by a survey of the forms of church structure which have predominated in successive periods of church history.[5] He acknowledges the great contribution of *The Structures of the Church* by Hans Küng in 1964 and then proceeds to analyze metropolitan, conciliar, denominational, and ecumenical structures which developed according to the needs of the church throughout the centuries.

Metropolitan Structures. Moody believes that the metropolitan church is the model from New Testament times to the Council of Nicea in A.D. 325. He finds this pattern in the New Testament, with the centrality of the Jerusalem Church in Luke-Acts as the foundation stone. In the Luke-Acts tradition Jerusalem was the only church until the founding of the church in Antioch (Acts 11:26).

The evidence for this argument is the consistent New Testament language which speaks of the "churches" in a Roman province or region but never uses the plural in regard to a single metropolitan area. We never read of the "churches of Jerusalem" or the "churches of Ephesus." Although there were certainly house churches and various groupings of believers in the larger cities, the New Testament writers thought of the church as singular in that metropolitan area. It is easy to see how such a view of the unity of the metropolitan church could quickly lead to a single metropolitan pastor or bishop-overseer.

Again it is possible to argue that this over-simplifies the situation and that with house churches, groups of Christians in the Roman armies, refugee churches in Pella and many other places, there were other patterns of church

---

[5]Ibid., 433-40. For Küng's contribution, see the English edition of Hans Küng, *The Structures of the Church* (South Bend: The University of Notre Dame Press, 1968).

structure. But Moody has the weight of both the New Testament and the church fathers in support of his claim that this is the dominant structure in the early centuries. This is another example of the value of his presupposition of diversity, for he finds evidence of diverse organizational patterns in the New Testament and is willing to allow a church to adapt the pattern which best responds to its historical circumstances. Bible and history both carry great weight here. History must always be criticized and corrected in the light of Holy Scripture, but we must also learn from history.

Conciliar Structures. The church council became the authority structure for all churches, beginning with the Council of Nicea in A.D. 325 and extending all the way to the Protestant Reformation of the sixteenth century. For Roman Catholics the conciliar pattern continued through the post-Reformation Council of Trent (1545-1563) and even through Vatican I (1869-1870) and Vatican II (1962-1965). This history included twenty-one ecumenical councils, the first eight in the East and the remainder in the West.

Again there were sectarians, Montanists, and assorted heretics, but the pattern of convening great ecumenical councils was intended precisely to deal with major issues such as conflicting views of Christ, the authority of the bishop, or the use of religious art in worship. Church leaders were trying to achieve a truly unified view on these matters in the church throughout the world. Moody stresses the fact that the church was responding to the challenge of its historical circumstances, primarily the shift from the Hebrew imagery of the biblical language to the philosophies of the Greek world. Even so, he finds the original pattern for the ecumenical council in the A.D. 49 Jerusalem Council of Acts 15, which was called to deal with the fundamental doctrinal issue as to whether Gentiles had to become circumcised Jews in order to become Christians. Incidentally, this first great doctrinal crisis arose in the church's *mission* to the Gentiles. Christianity would survive or perish on the basis of this decision!

Yet, with all its effort to achieve doctrinal unity, conciliarism has left the great rift between East and West, and the separation between Catholicism and Protestantism in the West. For Moody, and all others who take seriously the New Testament teachings on the one body of Christ, this Christian schism is a glaring contradiction. In addition, for one who sees the church primarily in terms of mission, it is the most threatening problem.

Denominational Structures. The denominational structures are rooted in the Protestant Reformation, but their proliferation into hundreds of separate organizations has been an embarrassment in the Protestant tradition. Although the free church pattern pre-dominated at the beginning, magnifying "the concept of the invisible body of Christ in the eucharist and in the *ekkelesia*," some of the reformers, out of the need to defend their movements, turned toward the idea of a state church defended by civil authority. Both Luther and Calvin, as well as their followers, took this path.

Moody believes that the free church tradition has never been given a fair opportunity to prove its benefits for the "churches and the Church." He wants to keep this vision before us and appeals to Christians "to turn again to the apostolic faith nurtured by the gathered company of committed believers who are willing to move away from national churches and become the pilgrim church again scattered throughout the world for witness, service and fellowship." It is not difficult to see that this is where Moody's heart is, but he is quite realistic in assessing the resistance of "anxious bishops and social activists and rigid conservatives" to the fulfillment of the vision.

Although Moody had named a fourth area of "ecumenical structures" as he projected this section of his ecclesiology, he does not treat that topic in a distinct section. Apparently he believes that the vision of the "gathered company of committed believers" still offers the best hope for ecumenical progress and is the line which he would like to see the churches pursue. Because he is a realist, he may also assume that several of the structures which have emerged in the history of Christianity may appear in different places in response to their historical circumstances.

To some it is an absolute anomaly that this man who was nurtured in the womb of Texas Baptists could be such a committed, activist, ecumenical Christian. Why is he not a narrow Baptist landmarker, anathematizing Catholics, fighting the Methodists, and wondering if anyone besides the Baptists will ever make it to heaven? No one can ever understand Moody's doctrine of the church without knowing the answer to that question. At the risk of being redundant let us point out once more the steps in his pilgrimage. Here are the crucial points.

(1) Moody began with the conviction that if we go back to the Scriptures and conform our doctrine and practice to their vision, we must find our unity in our One Lord.

(2) Because this longing for unity was the earnest prayer of Jesus, we cannot dismiss it and quietly accept the *status quo* of division and schism.

(3) When Moody boldly plunged into every possible ecumenical contact, studying in the Anglican "Meccas" of Oxford and Cambridge, teaching in the prestigious Pontifical Gregorian Institute in Rome, sharing in the colloquium of visiting scholars at the Ecumenical Institute in Jerusalem, he found the Holy Spirit confirming over and over again that we are indeed brothers and sisters in the one body of Christ.

(4) Even though the efforts to advance this invisible or spiritual unity in more visible ways were often frustrated by the opposition of "anxious bishops and rigid conservatives," Moody has clung to his hope that real progress

can be made. After all, if unity is the sovereign purpose of God, we must keep working at it and not despair.

As far as I can tell, this is about where Moody is at the present time. The only difference I can feel in his enthusiasm now and forty years ago is that he perhaps senses the road may be harder and the time required for the realization of the vision of our unity in the body of Christ may be longer than he might have thought in his youthful idealism. I know, however, that he has not given up, and that he is still as much at home in ecumenical worship in Latin, Greek, or Hebrew in Jerusalem as he is at Lonesome Dove church in Grapevine, Texas. The vision of unity has possessed him and will not let him go.

The Nature of the Church

With this topic we have come to a section of Moody's ecclesiology which has developed in several stages over more than thirty years. In a special edition of The Southern Baptist Theological Seminary faculty journal, *Review and Expositor,* honoring William Owen Carver, Moody published the views that comprise the first stage of his thought.[6] During the next two or three years the Seminary's president, Duke K. McCall, convened a seminar on the church composed of several of the members of the Seminary faculty and a few visiting scholars. Over several sessions many papers were submitted and discussed. Dale Moody and T. D. Price played a special role in collecting and screening these articles for later publication in *What Is the Church?*, edited by McCall.[7] The article went through a second stage of development for inclusion as a chapter in this symposium.[8] The final stage is found in Moody's theological *magnum opus, The Word of Truth.*[9]

It is especially instructive to see his sustained interest in this doctrine across the years and to evaluate the emphases which have been incorporated into its development. The basic structure has been the same from the beginning: the Church in relation to God, Jesus Christ, and the Holy Spirit. But, on the theological journey we see the origins of the visible-invisible church distinction and how, among other things, this entered into our Baptist confessions and saved many Baptists, and especially Southern Seminary, from being swamped by the "local church" exclusivism of Landmarkism. To J. R. Graves and J. M. Pendleton the expression "local church" was redundant; to them the local church was the only church. There would be no one church, incorporating all believers in the one body of Christ, until the heavenly assembly.

---

[6]"The Nature of the Church," *Rev Exp* 51:2 (April 1954): 204-16.

[7]Duke K. McCall, ed., *What Is the Church?* (Nashville: Broadman Press, 1958).

[8]"The Nature of the Church," ibid., 15-27.

[9]*Word of Truth,* 440-48.

Augustine's distinction between the earthly city (*civitas terrena*) and the heavenly city (*civitas Dei*) "has been perverted in Roman Catholicism by the identification of the historical institution with the heavenly ideal; yet for Augustine, the church, while participating in the *civitas Dei,* is not identical with the ideal until the end of history."[10] Calvin made a "strikingly similar" distinction with his view of the visible and invisible church. Moody traces this Calvinistic language about the nature of the church through the London Confession of Particular Baptists in 1644, to the Second Confession in 1677, through its adoption by Baptist associations in Philadelphia, Charleston, and Rhode Island. The priority of the spiritual or invisible organism over the institutional organization was obvious in all these confessions and was preserved with special clarity in the Abstract of Principles of Southern Seminary in 1858. Again Moody has demonstrated his deep commitment to understanding and evaluating the historical tradition and its impact upon our understanding of the church.

When we turn to the Trinitarian relationships of the church, we find the more typical biblical theology. In an exhaustive treatment that touches on almost every biblical reference to the church, Moody explores the church's relationship to God under the concepts of "people of God" and "temple of God." The church in relation to Christ is developed under the metaphors of the "body of Christ" and the "bride of Christ." The relationship to the Holy Spirit is also presented in two categories: the fellowship (*koinonia*) of the Spirit, which is summarized in the three terms, baptism, gift, and unity of the Spirit; and the ministry (*diakonia*) of the Spirit, which may also be summarized by the New Testament terms, the gifts (*charismata*) of the Spirit, the filling of the Spirit, and the sword of the Spirit.

There may be a conscious or unconscious influence of Karl Barth in this tightly-woven Trinitarian presentation of the doctrine of the church. In any case, Barth would applaud it, and it is certainly a powerful and compelling view of the nature of the church. It is rooted in the Scripture, developed in a Trinitarian theological context, and traced through a significant strand of church history. Light breaks in all directions in this presentation.

The Ministry of the Church

With this subject we enter an area of intense theological conflict. Moody sees the root of the problem in "the proper relation between the charismatic and official elements in the ministry of the New Testament church."[11] He finds room for the roots of all traditions from Quakerism to Catholicism in the New

---

[10]Ibid., 440.

[11]Ibid., 448.

Testament itself: "At one extreme is John and at the other are the Pastorals, with Paul at some point near the middle."[12]

After drawing an analogy between the ministry of Christ and the ministry of the church, he summarizes the ministry of the church under the New Testament terms *charismata* (the lists of spiritual gifts in 1 Corinthians 12:28-30, Romans 12:6-8, and Ephesians 4:11) and *cheirotonia* (the laying on of hands, or ordination). This is Moody's way of expressing the tension between the charismatic and official ministries. Deacons and elders (presbyters) are presented as the nearest thing to official ministers in the early church, with the special problem of *episcopos* or bishop arising in 1 Timothy 3:1, where the bishop-overseer may be an elder who is elevated to a role that is distinct from the other elders.

The Ministry of Women. Moody uses both Scripture and early church history to support his claim that "in the early church three orders of women developed along with the three orders of men."[13] These three ministries of deaconesses, virgins, and widows were vital in the early church, and in 1 Timothy 5:3-16 more is said about the role of widows than about deacons, presbyters, or bishops!

Although Moody does not make a case for the ordination of women, he does claim that they "were in other ways marked off by functions not expected of all Christians."

Initiation into the Church: Baptism

Moody explains his intention in this treatment: "It is the purpose of this brief essay to point out the factors that focus on the most appropriate time for the administration of baptism and the primacy of faith in baptismal theology. The priority of grace to faith is presupposed."[14] With that he launches a study of those baptismal theologies which link baptism and purification. Although this association may be found in the baptism of John the Baptist, his strong emphasis on the confession of sins "leaves no room for the baptism of those void of repentance and faith."[15] Moody especially deplores the linking of infant baptism with the idea of original guilt. He acknowledges the growing practice of pedobaptism among Baptists which may "make room for the faith of innocent children, who later appropriate their baptism, but it is doubtful that it can pass for a repentance baptism that involves guilt and forgiveness."[16]

---

[12]Ibid., 449.

[13]Ibid., 549.

[14]Ibid., 460.

[15]Ibid., 461.

[16]Ibid., 463.

Because Luke does not use the metaphor "body of Christ," Moody treats the baptismal formulae in Acts as "identification" with Christ rather than as "incorporation" into the body of Christ, an expression characteristic of Paul. In his consideration of baptism and regeneration, salvation, and illumination, Moody finds three further approaches in which the primacy of faith is assumed in baptismal theology.

Although Moody stoutly defends the primacy of faith in baptismal theology, he unleashed something of a storm in Southern Baptist circles by quoting British Baptists and Disciples of Christ in the United States who propose that both infant baptism and believers' baptism be accepted as alternative practices in a united church. He admits that "as an interim solution toward organic unity this may be the only way."[17] This proposal and comment are found in Moody's 1967 monograph, *Baptism: Foundation for Christian Unity*. He makes the very practical observation that in such a situation believers' baptism would predominate in missionary situations where those outside Christian households were being reached, while infant or child baptism would predominate in families traditionally Christian. But, with all his love for the vision of church unity, he finds reunion of limited value if it does not involve radical reform in the theology and practice of baptism.

Fellowship in the Church: The Lord's Supper

After a survey of the wide variations in the observance of the Lord's Supper, Moody traces the origins of this church practice to the Jewish Passover, the Last Supper of Jesus with his disciples (the major source), and to its shaping in the *Agape* or Love Feast in the early church (Jude 12). He finds its significance in the biblical words used for the Supper, six of which words he groups by pairs under the three tenses: the present significance is expressed in the words *eucharistia* (thanksgiving) and *koinonia* (fellowship or participation); the past significance is brought out by the words "covenant" and "remembrance"; the future significance is expressed by the terms "Kingdom of God" and "the coming of Christ." The fractious debates in church history over the exact forms of the bread and the cup, as well as the frequency of observance, are briefly surveyed. For Moody, what the Supper proclaims is primary, regardless of the frequency of observance or the forms of the elements.

---

[17](Philadelphia: The Westminster Press, 1967) 303. This work grew out of Moody's doctoral dissertation at Oxford University and was undoubtedly one of the reasons for the unprecedented invitation to a Baptist to teach theology at the Gregorian Institute in Rome.

The Worship of the Church

The final section of Moody's ecclesiology involves a study of the biblical sources and the historical types of Christian worship. Although he describes many specific forms, such as cultic shrines in the patriarchal period, sacrifices and festivals in ancient Israel, Pauline collections, service, and ministry in the Spirit, he finds the most fundamental thing in Christian worship to be the gathering together "to celebrate the acts of God in creation and redemption."[18] After presenting the major historical types of sacrifice in the Catholic Mass and the centrality of the Scripture in Calvin and the Reformers, Moody calls for more freedom for true spiritual worship. He closes on the note with which he began: the mission of the church can be realized only with a renewed vitality of worship.

CONCLUDING EVALUATION

Although we have evaluated this systematic statement of Moody's ecclesiology at each point in our brief exposition, it may be well to conclude with an evaluation of the entire picture and Moody's personal pilgrimage in formulating it. The ecumenical vision of the 1940s and 1950s has not been realized; but significant things have been achieved, and there are certainly more to come. Now in his seventies, Moody can look back with joy and thanksgiving upon changes in church doctrine and practice, to which he has made no small contribution. Let us note some of these.

(1) With a seriousness which could not have been imagined a generation or two ago, all across the theological spectrum from Catholicism to Pentecostalism the intensive study of the Bible is bringing about renewed vitality, challenge to church traditions, and new motivation for Christian mission. Moody has pioneered in this all his life, and it may explain the fact that the fruits of this biblical research in his systematic theology are studied in theological schools all the way from the Gregorian Institute in Rome to the Criswell Institute in Dallas. No matter how far we have to go, the pattern of creative biblical study has been set. We will see new light continually breaking forth in all Christian traditions.

(2) The isolation and segregation of Christian scholars and traditions from one another has been broken down. This movement began long before our generation, and it has many causes. But few scholars have taken advantage

---

[18]*Word of Truth,* 474. In support of this viewpoint Moody cites Ferdinand Hahn, *The Worship of the Early Church,* trans. David E. Green (Philadelphia: The Fortress Press, 1973), 36; and Eduard Schweizer, *Divine Service in the New Testament* (Montreal: The Presbyterian College, 1970), 15.

of this opportunity as well as Dale Moody. He has become a familiar figure in monasteries, universities, libraries, cathedrals, and ecumenical institutes across the world. His personal friendships with leading scholars across the theological spectrum have enriched his own theology and contributed to theirs. They are often surprised to find him a walking encyclopedia, not only of biblical and Baptist theology, but also of their own traditions.

This free exchange and association between Christians and scholars of all communions is another pattern that has been set. We can never go back. It may offer, in the long run, our greatest hope for deeper understanding and unity in the body of Christ. We may find that it is more important to live together, worship together, and study together than it is to sign a common theological confession!

(3) For thousands of theological students this broad acquaintance with such a wide spectrum of Christian writers has opened vistas which they could never have imagined. It enriches understanding, fellowship, worship, and the sense of Christian mission in today's world. Although Moody's students may have hated at examination time the vast bibliography his approach required, they could never go back into a narrow isolationism once they got their blinders off and saw the wider vistas he afforded them. Even when Moody did not succeed in converting a student to his own theological position, he often launched him on an exciting lifelong theological quest.

(4) One of the most important contributions of this type of ecclesiology is its impact upon the restorationist movements. From the Radical Reformation to the present time, various church groups have attempted to restore the New Testament pattern and call all Christians to follow them. Moody and other scholars have demonstrated conclusively that multiple patterns were emerging in the New Testament period. Although this has been threatening to many in his own Baptist tradition, this is probably his greatest contribution to the Baptist heritage in which he was nurtured. It simply cannot be maintained that one church has the truth and all others must acknowledge it. Taken seriously, this approach deals a death blow to the Landmarkism which has threatened for more than a century to take over the Southern Baptist tradition. Along with his lifetime dedication to the dismantling of hyper-Calvinism, Moody has been an implacable foe of Landmark Baptist successionism. This contribution will influence his own denomination long after he has passed from the scene.

It seems appropriate to conclude this evaluation by emphasizing a perspective which pervades Moody's ecclesiology from beginning to end. We may call it an eschatological perspective. Rooted in the Scriptures, the church is always the dynamic community of the Spirit moving on toward the future goal. It will have to go through many changes and adapt to many challenges. But we can trust the Holy Spirit to guide the church if we keep coming back to the Holy Scripture to test and correct both theology and practice. This fidelity to the authority of Scripture leaves an unresolved barrier between Moody's theology and the Catholic theology which gives an equal authority to tradition. As we have seen, Moody respects the many historical traditions which have shaped the church, but he never has granted an authority to tradition which matches the authority of Scripture. All tradition must be evaluated and challenged in the light of Scripture, and that is a never-ending task.

Christians are called, then, to a journey which will see dynamic growth and change until they are gathered into that ''general assembly and church of the firstborn'' in heaven. Even then the vista is open-ended for all eternity as we are changed into Christ's image ''from glory into glory''!

THEOLOGY, CHRISTOLOGY, AND ESCHATOLOGY

E. FRANK TUPPER
THE SOUTHERN BAPTIST THEOLOGICAL SEMINARY
LOUISVILLE KY 40280

In 1964 Jürgen Moltmann published *Theologie der Hoffnung*,[1] Wolfhart Pannenberg *Grundzüge der Christologie*,[2] and Dale Moody *The Hope of Glory*.[3] These three different books together represent the creative correlation of theology, christology, and eschatology. Moltmann formulated a theology of promise and fulfillment, thoroughly informed by an eschatological understanding of God as "the God of hope." Pannenberg explored the foundations of christology "from below" which rooted in Jesus' eschatological mission in behalf of the Kingdom of God and its proleptic fulfillment in Jesus' singular resurrection destiny. Moody expounded his understanding of the biblical teachings on eschatology in terms of the hope of humanity, the hope of history, and the hope of creation. All three theologians opted for an eschatological horizon, wherein the vision of God, the story of Jesus, and the vitality of hope converge. As Moody put it, "All theology and Christology are ultimately eschatology."[4]

---

[1]Jürgen Moltmann, *Theology of Hope,* trans. James W. Leitch (London: SCM Press, 1967).

[2]Wolfhart Pannenberg, *Jesus—God and Man,* trans. Lewis L. Wilkins and Duane A. Priebe (Philadelphia: The Westminster Press, 1968).

[3]Dale Moody, *The Hope of Glory* (Grand Rapids, MI: William B. Eerdmans Publishing Co., 1964).

[4]Ibid., 15.

FROM 1964 TO 1984

Much has happened since 1964, the stuff of which books are written and libraries are made. The advance toward "the Great Society" collapsed in the fiery smoke of blackened ghettoes in the urban centers across America. The cycle of poverty, joblessness, family disintegration and despair smolders with an even greater potential for explosion in Ronald Reagan's America. The disastrous war in Vietnam has left a bloody stain on American hands—hands that gave up "the brightest and the best" to bombardment of unprecedented destruction that now too many want to forget (and almost have: Nicaragua, Honduras, El Salvador).

Tanks from the Soviet bloc rolled into Czechoslovakia, ending the Dubček experiment of "socialism with a human face." The winds of freedom blew in Poland for a season, but "Solidarity" suffocated from Russian repression—a martyred young priest a symbol of the powerlessness of the church in the homeland of Pope John Paul II. Although Alexander Solzhenitsyn chronicled the story of the harsh reality of community tyranny in *Gulag Archipelago, 1918-1956*, the Russian invasion of Afghanistan has reasserted the legitimate reasons to fear the Kremlin.

Millions of starving children have died in the long famine stretching across northern Africa, and the world of plenty congratulated itself for giving a Band-Aid to cover their graves. *Apartheid* is a globally-recognized word which names the intransigent and tragic racism of South Africa, but it conceals the systemic racism of every industrialized nation of the West: Jim Crow is not dead, only more sophisticated, out of the alleys in white sheets and onto the streets where money speaks. Warnings have just begun to crack the apathy surrounding AIDS, a viral pestilence of immeasurable global proportions— the shadow of "the fourth horseman of the Apocalypse" looming on the horizon of the twenty-first century.

Egyptian President Anwar Sadat took a bold journey to Jerusalem for the sake of peace, but his assassinated hopes are largely splattered in terrorist blood all over the Middle East. Peace with Israel requires a place for the Palestinians, but the dispossessed seem doomed to remain displaced.

American astronauts have walked safely on the moon—"One short step for a man, a giant step forward for mankind"—but a step toward what? Space threatens to become another arena of military conflict for the superpowers. The promise of "Star Wars" may silence talks at the peace table, with NATO armed for the first time with nuclear missiles. Children are now heard to say— not "When I grow up," but "If I grow up, I want to be. . . . " With ever increasing frequency parents have to answer the question of their little ones: "What should I do in a nuclear war, Mommy?"

The Holocaust has twin reference points, one in the past, the other in the future: *Auschwitz,* the who-would-have-ever-thought-it-possible extermination of six million Jews in Nazi Germany, half the Jewish population in the world; *Nuclear Winter,* "the day after" nuclear war, which threatens the very possibility of life on planet Earth. The logic of Hiroshima shrivels in the lunacy of Nagasaki, an ever present reminder that someone will use all the weapons available to humiliate the enemy and . . . end . . . war.

Much has happened from 1964 to 1984 until now. Is the situation two decades beyond 1964 any different from the two decades prior to 1964? Is 1984 really different from 1944? Would world history have looked less violent, less tragic in 1944 than in 1984? Two epochal differences have appeared: the Holocaust and the Bomb. Yet theology has hardly begun to comprehend what these events mean for "theology" (though Moltmann's *The Crucified God* marked a turning point in 1973). The human situation in "1984" is different from 1964. How should theological reflection occur today? Where does theologizing most appropriately happen today? What posture should characterize a theologian at work today? These are difficult questions, and far more than simply methodological problems.

THEOLOGY TRACKING SPIRITUALITY

Henri Nouwen, who reaches for the depths and walks the frontiers of Christian spirituality, has identified a new kind of person from the 1970s side of 1964—"nuclear man." Nouwen described him as a prisoner of the present without meaningful connections with his past or future. "If there is anything worthwhile in life it must be here and now."[5] Not every young person is "nuclear," however, and older people are not inevitably prenuclear. The difference is not in age but in consciousness and life style. According to Nouwen, "nuclear man" is the person "who realizes that his creative powers hold the potential for self-destruction."

> He sees that in this nuclear age vast new industrial complexes enable man to produce in one hour that which he labored over for years in the past, but he also . . . suffers from the inevitable knowledge that his time is a time in which it has become possible for man to destroy not only life but also the possibility of rebirth, not only man but also mankind, not only periods of existence but also history itself. *For nuclear man the future has become an option.*[6]

---

[5]Henry J. M. Nouwen, *The Wounded Healer* (Garden City NY: Doubleday & Company, 1972; 1979) 4.

[6]Ibid., 6-7. Italics not in original.

Of course, people have always been aware of the paradox wherein life and death touch each other in morbid and fragile ways. Previously, however, they have been able to adapt the new situation to an earlier optimistic perspective. For "nuclear man," Nouwen insists, this new knowledge cannot be channeled through old insights, because it radically and definitively disrupts all existing frames of reference. *"For him, the problem is not that the future holds a new danger, such as nuclear war, but that there might be no future at all."*[7]

The plight of nuclear man is Nouwen's graphic depiction of the suffering world, and it leads him to a powerful description of the condition of all humanity in life and death. Although many words are available to name our common human brokenness, Nouwen considers "loneliness" the best expression of the depths of human need, the universal human woundedness which theology and ministry should address. Yet he surprisingly concludes: "The Christian way of life does not take away our gift [!] of loneliness; it protects and cherishes it as a precious gift."[8] Why? The separation and incompletion that we all feel, our inevitable lonely conditions, reveal our need for God, for grace, for a future in God's grace. What does theology mean for the more or less, now and then "nuclear man," the inevitably wounded person who suffers "loneliness"?

Loneliness implies absence. Enter Martin Marty, church historian turned contemporary theologian, with *A Cry of Absence: Reflections for the Winter of the Heart.*[9] He invites the reader to undertake a journey of the soul in the face of the threat of death. The winter image represents death, and death occasions "a wintry Absence, Absence in the heart." Whatever the climate, the heart cannot escape the chill of winter. "When death comes, when absence creates pain—then anyone can anticipate the season of cold."[10] He adds pointedly: "The absence can also come, however, to a waste space left when the divine is distant, the sacred is remote, when God is silent."[11] The weather may change, but the bleakness of the soul remains.

Marty follows the Roman Catholic theologian Karl Rahner in distinguishing two kinds of spirituality: a summery style of spirituality and a wintry

----

[7]Ibid., 7. Italics not in original.

[8]Ibid., 84.

[9]Martin E. Marty, *A Cry of Absence: Reflections for the Winter of the Heart* (San Francisco: Harper & Row, 1983).

[10]Ibid., 2.

[11]Ibid.

sort of spirituality.[12] Summery spirituality sings in the warm immediacy of God's Presence, a Presence of peace and joy. Brilliant and radiant sunshine dispel all shadows. Wintry spirituality wrestles with the Absence of God, the absence of Presence, the barrenness and bleakness of abandonment. Sunshine cannot dispel or deny or justify the dark shadows which loom over the whole of life. Though both types are needed and neither is chemically pure, Rahner thinks that the church should not place all its hopes in the summery type: "The Church has to think more than it has previously done about how to frame its message for men who are troubled, but who in the end have a faith which is certainly not strengthened by a spirituality of the charismatic type."[13]

This type, according to Rahner, "would be made up of those who, although they are committed Christians who pray and receive the sacraments, nevertheless find themselves at home in a wintry sort of spirituality, in which they stand alongside the atheist, but obviously without becoming atheists themselves."[14] While they do face the same horizon, believers of the wintry sort are not atheists "who have excluded God from their horizon." The church must take this wintry type seriously: "To it belong all those who have gone through all the purgatories and hells of modern rationalism."[15] Here Marty believes that Rahner may have unwittingly limited wintry spirituality to intellectuals. Sometimes people have become disillusioned, doubting and despairing because they have had what might be called "the modern experience, and therefore have been unable to include God in their horizon."[16] Whatever the definition, Rahner's winterers experience an horizon from which God has been excluded or from which God has chosen to be excluded, but they remain committed Christians, *troubled, but Christians who in the end have a faith.* These wintry Christians know the limits of reason, the loneliness of a godless horizon, the chill of winter with its cry of Absence, Absence.

Searching for a text for the wintry way—a piety for the not naturally pious—Marty reaches for one corner of the Bible, the Book of Psalms. The Psalms, the church's hymn book and prayer book, have the clearest claim for a spirituality based on the Hebrew and Christian traditions. Yet they do not simply match contemporary experience: "God is near in the summery psalms

---

[12]Ibid., 5-13. See "Interview with Karl Rahner," *The Month,* 2nd New Series 7:7 (July 1974), 637-45, esp. 641. Marty coins the phrase "summery spirituality," whereas Rahner speaks of "the charismatic type."

[13]Marty, 11.

[14]Ibid., 12.

[15]Ibid.

[16]Ibid., 86.

in ways that few experience the immediacy of today, or remote in wintry ones to the point of denial and threat."[17] Marty speaks a personal word:

> Through recent years of ransacking and personal plundering, something occurred in my reading that made me associate the psalms with Rahner's wintry sort of spirituality. So in my notebooks that grew up not on my scholarly desk . . . but from bedside, sickroom, or island and desert reading, I began to take notice. Is this psalm more appropriate to the summery or wintry, the sunny or the windswept spirituality? . . . To my surprise I noticed that more than half the psalms had as their major burden or content life on the wintry landscape of the heart. Many more contained extensive references to the spiritual terrain of winter, even if it did not predominate. Only about a third of the psalms were, indeed, the simple property of those for whom the summery style would exhaust Christian spirituality.[18]

A wintry spirituality which shares the horizon near where the godless live struggles with elusive mysteries: the mystery of death and the mystery of evil. Marty says: "The search for a piety does not permit evasion of the central issue of life: its 'being toward death.' "[19] Every Yes to life has to be made in the face of this "ceasing to be." Those whose horizon excludes God are aware of death but are unable to say "Yes" in the face of it. Whoever says "God" has chosen to affirm "goodness and power," and the affirmation bristles with all kinds of questions. Why death? Why the pain and suffering which so often comes with death? Did God cause death? Could God stop death? Whatever the questions, the Psalms know: death remains. The Hebrews mourned the dead, but their stories of mourning never include "a consoling cleric who enters the room of mourners late at night to give pat answers to the question, 'Why?' "[20] In the Psalms death is not simply evil; like winter, death belongs to the rhythm of life. Accordingly, the Psalms do not offer the comfort and promise of an afterlife; Sheol is more an unattractive after-*death*. Actually Marty hears a startling "Yes" to death in the depths of Hebrew piety: "The writers of the psalms confronted death but saw through it to life because in death they saw God."[21]

The mystery of evil intensifies the mystery of death. Why do the righteous suffer? Why do children die? Why does life go wrong? "The mystery of why evil seems built into the structure and pattern of ordinary events is a spiritual problem,"[22] Marty claims (a theological one as well, I would ar-

---

[17]Ibid., 36.

[18]Ibid., 39.

[19]Ibid., 53.

[20]Ibid., 63.

[21]Ibid., 58.

[22]Ibid., 78-79.

gue). These ancient questions about evil cause doubt, and they strike with bitter force whenever one realizes the answers are as distant as ever. Contact. A wintry spirituality walks on the bleak landscape with those who have excluded God from their horizon on these very grounds. The deniers act with intuition and intelligence. "You can feel the unfairness of life in the bones, and you can reason your way to see it if eyes are open and minds clear."[23]

Marty is starkest when he talks about "the season of abandonment." He speaks eloquently and passionately of Jesus' abandonment: "Then, in the soul's dark night and the heart's deep winter, comes the recall of a shriek or groan more intense than all the others. The quotation on the cross comes from the psalms, and I can never let it go: *My God, my God, why hast thou forsaken me?*' "[24] Some commentators eliminate Jesus' abandonment at the cross, because the quotation from the beginning of Psalm 22 implied the Psalm's positive ending. Their pious interpretation turns the death-cry of Jesus into an affirmation of faith. Marty's response is caustic. What they offer has little to do with agonies in the garden, the drinking of bitter cups, or the hope of Easter dawn. In this plot the point really is that Jesus experienced abandonment. Jesus cried out because a pledge seemed to be broken, and it was being broken. Jesus was not supposed to be abandoned but abandoned he was. Marty is poignant: " 'The cry of dereliction': under that term his shout enters the list of classic phrases. There are derelict ships and there was a derelict Son of God."[25] In the Gospel story Marty affirms a trustworthy God is behind it all. He writes: "The crucified victim was the *only* forsaken one, the true derelict. The rest of us die in company, in *his* company. God certified his gift and his act and 'raised him up.' Never again is aloneness to be so stark for others."[26]

The horizon seems the same, but trust and hope grow. Marty the winterer knows occasions when Absence leaves the horizon and Presence occurs: "One might speak of this Presence on the horizon as being touchable in its impending nearness: here is what may be called the 'palpabilification' of God."[27] These words appear to fuse the horizon of the Psalms with the horizon of the Gospel, of promise. So Marty ends this journey of the soul on a surprising note: "One hopes."[28]

---

[23]Ibid., 79.

[24]Ibid., 134-35.

[25]Ibid., 136-37.

[26]Ibid., 139.

[27]Ibid., 172.

[28]Ibid.

With deep insight, unusual candor, and sometimes unguarded passion Martin Marty has characterized the situation of the Christian theologian today: the necessity to do theology in the midst of the inexplicable brokenness of life and before the inevitability and finality of death. Two questions must be put to Marty and to all wintry believers: (1) Do the Psalms contextualize and demythologize the Gospel story, or do the Gospel narratives re-contextualize and remythologize the Psalms? (2) Is the God one meets in the Psalms actually defined anew in the story of Jesus, the Abba-Father whose Kingdom will come? Or, is the God one meets in the Psalms only experienced afresh, the Presence of God's ever impending nearness through the story of Jesus? These interrelated questions accentuate what Marty already knows: everything turns on the character and identity of God.

PARENTHESIS ON METHOD

Theology, using the texts of Holy Scripture, must be done today with life face to face with death, and death face to face with life. The arena for testing eschatological hope is the valley of the shadow of death, the edge of the abyss of Nothingness, the horizon of Godforsakenness. The threat of the cold of winter is not new, but the possibility of the cold night of a nuclear winter is. Death remains the testing ground of eschatology, of hope against hope, but now the testing ground encompasses the whole earth simultaneously. The situation is different but strangely the same. The possibility of a nuclear Holocaust intensifies the issue of eschatology, but the problem remains preeminently personal in the contemplation of "ceasing to be." Put bluntly and probably badly, the issue is "the resurrection of the Crucified." Put differently but certainly not adequately, the issue is the "abandonment" of Jesus on the cross. Theology and anthropology notwithstanding, eschatology finally turns on the hinge of christology. The story of Jesus is decisive for one's approach to and understanding of eschatology.

Two theologians stand out today for their creative and constructive approaches to the enterprise of christology: Wolfhart Pannenberg and Edward Schillebeeckx. Each has a distinctive understanding of the story of Jesus, which includes different but affirmative interpretations of the death and resurrection of Jesus—especially his resurrection. Focusing on their understanding of the death and resurrection of Jesus fails to do justice to their larger christological proposals; nevertheless, the concern of the remainder of this essay will concentrate on how the interpretation of the death and resurrection of Jesus shapes theological perspective on death and hope for eternal life.

THE DEATH AND RESURRECTION OF JESUS:
WOLFHART PANNENBERG

In *Jesus—God and Man* Pannenberg moved the discussion of christology to a new stage, correlating Jesus' eschatological proclamation of the Kingdom of God with the historicality of Jesus' singular resurrection. Pannenberg's proposal (elaborated and refined) embraces a complicated but cohesive pattern of thought, but relevant elements for the purpose of this essay can be identified and highlighted.

1. Jesus proclaimed the imminent nearness of the Kingdom of God in the context of apocalyptic expectation of the end of the world. Yet Jesus claimed that the presence of God's future salvation had already happened through him in advance, the presence of God's love. The future and the present are inextricably interwoven, but Pannenberg emphasizes: "Jesus underscored the *present impact* of the imminent future."[29] This tension between the futurity of the Kingdom and its present arrival in Jesus underscores the proleptic character of his claim: Jesus' entire activity about God's inbreaking Kingdom required God's future confirmation. Pannenberg says bluntly: "The question about such a future confirmation of Jesus' claim by God himself is held open by the temporal difference between the beginning of God's rule, which was already present in Jesus' activity, and its future fulfillment with the coming Son of Man on the clouds of heaven."[30] While Jesus' mighty deeds could partially authenticate his claim of authority, even the disciples could follow Jesus only in anticipation of future confirmation by God. Since Jesus expected the end to occur in the near future, Jesus could force a confrontation in Jerusalem without despair. God would vindicate him whether he had to endure death before the end came or not.

2. Pannenberg maintains that Jesus' conflict with the Jewish authorities, who had absolutized the Law as the criterion of salvation, constitutes the essential reason for his condemnation as a blasphemer by the Sanhedrin and his crucifixion by the Romans on the slanderous charge of sedition. Proclaiming the nearness of the Kingdom of God and offering eschatological salvation, Jesus set himself above the Law of Moses and essentially claimed authority belonging only to God. This claim lay behind the Jewish condemnation of Jesus. While the indictment against Jesus probably involved some concrete incident, Pannenberg says: "The reproach of blasphemy (Mark 14:64) through

---

[29]Wolfhart Pannenberg, *Theology and the Kingdom of God* (Philadelphia: The Westminster Press, 1969) 53.

[30]Pannenberg, *Jesus—God and Man*, 65.

the claim of an authority properly belonging only to God was probably the real reason why the Jewish authorities took action against Jesus, regardless of what pretexts may have been in the indictment itself.''[31]

Although Jesus continued to believe in the vindication of his mission—despite attacks of doubt and threats of despair—the condemnation of Jesus to death for blasphemy and subsequent execution for treason constituted nothing less than a disaster for Jesus personally and for his disciples vocationally. The disciples fled to Galilee, because the condemnation of Jesus in God's own name destroyed the foundations of discipleship. Jesus ''suffered the abandonment of God in death.''[32] He alone died completely forsaken, Godforsaken. Pannenberg says:

> To be excluded from God's nearness in spite of clear consciousness of it would be hell. This element agrees remarkably with the situation of Jesus' death: as the one who proclaimed and lived the eschatological nearness of God, Jesus died the death of one rejected.[33]

How he could bear this contradiction is beyond comprehension. Precisely in his dedication to God's will in the darkness of the cross—which meant the failure of his mission—Jesus' dedication to God took the form of self-sacrifice.[34]

3. Jesus' proclamation of the imminent end did not fail but was surprisingly confirmed in his own person, that is, Jesus' singular resurrection from the dead. Pannenberg concedes some difficulty in this explanation. Since no one witnessed the event of resurrection itself, speaking about the resurrection rests on an *inference* from the appearances of the living Jesus, who had been killed and buried but did not remain dead. These appearances of the once dead but now alive Jesus evoked the unprecedented conclusion, ''Jesus is risen from the dead.'' Yet this conclusion is not an arbitrary or exchangeable interpretation. ''On the contrary,'' Pannenberg says,

> the inference has an inner necessity: If Jesus (after he was dead) now lives, then he was—before he was seen for the first time as the living One—either resuscitated or, conversely (when the mode of his contemporary life excludes resuscitation and his death was undoubtedly certain), he has been transformed into another ''life.''[35]

---

[31]Ibid., 252.

[32]Ibid., 261.

[33]Ibid., 271.

[34]Ibid., 334.

[35]Wolfhart Pannenberg, ''Dogmatische Erwägungen zur Auferstehung Jesu,'' *Kerygma und Dogma*, 14(1968): 111.

In this context "life" is a metaphor, but it is an irreplaceable metaphor, because resurrection refers to an event which happened to Jesus who had died yet now lives, without being able to say exactly what the word "life" means. The disciples used the apocalyptic category of "resurrection" to characterize this new life of Jesus, but their application of the category represented a radical departure from the apocalyptic traditions which anticipated a general "resurrection of the dead" only at the end of history. Pannenberg says: "Evidently something had happened to the witnesses of the appearances of the Risen One for which their language had no other word than that used to characterize the eschatological expectation, i. e., resurrection from the dead."[36] If God raised Jesus from the dead, Pannenberg concludes, the resurrection means that the end of the world has already begun, that God has confirmed the pre-Easter activity of Jesus, and that God is revealed definitively in the eschatological history of Jesus Christ.

4. The tradition of the appearances of the resurrected Lord and the tradition of the empty tomb emerged independently and remain separate in the oldest strata of tradition, 1 Corinthians 15 and Mark 16 respectively. Since the appearances reported in the Gospels reflect the legendary development and later integration of these two traditions, Pannenberg concentrates the historical question of the appearances of the risen Jesus entirely on 1 Corinthians 15:1-11. Clearly intending to give proof for the facticity of the resurrection by means of witnesses who are subject to interrogation, Paul appeals to a formulated tradition which emerged even prior to Paul's visit to Jerusalem—more or less contemporary with the death of Jesus. Pannenberg concludes:

> In view of the age of the formulated traditions used by Paul and the proximity of Paul to the events, the assumption that the appearances of the resurrected Lord were really experienced by a number of members of the primitive Christian community and not perhaps invented in the course of later legendary development has a good foundation.[37]

Pannenberg will characterize the mode of the appearances as "an extraordinary vision," because it would not be visible to everyone. Yet primitive Christianity certainly knew how to distinguish between ecstatic visionary experiences and encounters with the resurrected Lord. Pannenberg insists: "The Easter appearances are not to be explained from the Easter faith of the disciples; rather, conversely, the Easter faith of the disciples is to be explained from the appearances."[38] The logic, the number, and the distribution

---

[36]Wolfhart Pannenberg, "The Revelation of God in Jesus of Nazareth," *Theology as History,* ed. James M. Robinson and John B. Cobb, Jr., vol. 3 of *New Frontiers in Theology* (New York: Harper & Row, 1967) 115.

[37]Pannenberg, *Jesus—God and Man,* 91.

[38]Ibid., 96.

of the appearances excludes the explanation of the "subjective vision hypothesis."

Though the results of the discussion of the appearances are valid apart from the judgment of the empty tomb, Pannenberg thinks the historicity of the tradition of the empty tomb is significant for the final conclusion. The Christian community in Jerusalem could hardly have proclaimed Jesus' resurrection without a reliable testimony for the empty tomb. Moreover, early Jewish polemic against the Christian message of Jesus' resurrection acknowledged the empty tomb but offered a different explanation for it. The tradition of the empty tomb emerged independently of the tradition of the appearances and corroborated the truth of the resurrection of Jesus.[39]

5. While the final substantiation of Jesus' resurrection awaits eschatological verification, Pannenberg insists that historical-critical investigation of the reports of the resurrection of Jesus is finally inescapable. His arguments for the historicity of Jesus' resurrection can be put briefly: (a) The resurrection of Jesus happened to him and constitutes the presupposition for his appearances as well as the explanation of the empty tomb. (b) The resurrection of Jesus occurred at a specific time and a specific place—essential characteristics of an historical event. (c) The reports of the resurrection of Jesus are subject to historical-critical research; otherwise, the historical claim of the eventness of Jesus' resurrection would be forfeited. (d) The resurrection of Jesus is an event unlike all other events, but the appearances of the risen Jesus—expressible only in metaphor—are appropriate subjects for historical inquiry. The resurrection of Jesus is "at least" but always "more than" an historical event. Thus the resurrection of Jesus, though subject to historical-critical research in its eventness, does not permit an indisputable historical judgment. It remains opaque. Pannenberg argues that the historian, nevertheless, has something quite positive and theologically significant to say:

> An event has happened, whose more detailed qualities evade his judgment
> . . . [but] it is an event which relates to Jesus, and indeed, the dead Jesus—
> an event which in any case means that Jesus thereafter was no longer dead.
> With so critically delimited a statement, which in spite of its negative form
> is eminently positive through the exactness of its negation, history guards
> the mystery of the resurrection of Jesus.[40]

6. Pannenberg has always linked the resurrection of Jesus with his eschatological proclamation of the Kingdom of God on the one side and the future destiny of humanity on the other. The yearning of humanity strains for fulfillment in an ideal community beyond the brokenness of earthly life. Hu-

---

[39]Ibid., 101-105.

[40]Pannenberg, "Dogmatische Erwägungen," 112-13.

manity's search for fulfillment lacks a conclusive answer within this life, and death renders this search meaningless. So reflection on human destiny leads to thought beyond this world to God and compels the contemplation of "life beyond death." For Pannenberg the hope for eternal life is fundamental to the very definition of "humanness."[41] In fact, this anthropological truth, which converges with the horizon of apocalyptic expectation and nurtures hope for eternal life, is essential to Pannenberg's entire theology. In the light of this theological anthropology, Pannenberg has sketched in various writings the elements of his own eschatological proposal: he did so as early as 1962 in *What Is Man?* and as recently as 1984 with his Ingersoll Lecture on Immortality at Harvard Divinity School, "Constructive and Critical Functions of Christian Eschatology."

Amid the brokenness of life in this world, however, the issue is not only the question of human destiny but also the question of God. In the face of atheistic challenge Pannenberg concedes: "Hence only the full manifestation of God's kingdom in the future—which at the same time will bring about the definite realization of human destiny and thus the final reconciliation of God with his creation—can finally decide the reality of God."[42] Yet the difference between the eschatological future of God and the present condition of life in the world does not preclude the experience of God's future in the present. Pannenberg says:

> Eschatological hope empowers the individual to carry the burden of its finite existence with all its irremovable limitations and disgraceful frustrations. It encourages the human person to face the evils of this present world as they are, without illusion. Hope in a transcendent completion of human existence in communion with God illumines the present existence despite its shortcomings. It can liberate a person to give thanks to God in the midst of suffering and death. Thus in some way the eternal destiny of the human creature can be felt to be already present in this life, and such presence can become a source of happiness and joy.[43]

Only through probing the limitations of Pannenberg's presentation can the potential and value of his proposal for Christian eschatology be determined. The validity of his interpretation of the death and resurrection of Jesus cannot be seen apart from the vulnerability of his arguments.

---

[41]See Wolfhart Pannenberg, *What Is Man?* (Philadelphia: Fortress Press, 1970) 41-53.

[42]Wolfhart Pannenberg, "Can Christianity Do without an Eschatology," *The Christian Hope,* by C. B. Caird and others, No. 3 of *Theological Collections* (London: SPCK, 1970) 31.

[43]Wolfhart Pannenberg, "Constructive and Critical Functions of Christian Eschatology," *HTR* 77:2 (1984): 124.

1. Pannenberg's creative and venturesome christology "from below" builds upon careful but minimal [!] foundations in the history of Jesus. In comparison Schillebeeckx's massive examination of the different dimensions of Jesus' proclamation and activity indicates how much of the Jesus tradition Pannenberg has yet to appropriate. The underlying issue critical for Christian theology is the relationship of eschatology and ethics. Pannenberg emphasizes that Jesus' conflict with the Law and his subsequent condemnation for blasphemy remain the motivating factors behind his crucifixion, but Pannenberg (and Schillebeeckx) minimize the intrinsic political significance of Jesus' ministry and the threat he represented to the Roman occupying army. Jürgen Moltmann's attention to the similarities and dissimilarities between Jesus and the Zealots in the politically-charged situation in Palestine and Jesus' "understandable" execution as a rebel[44] relates the horizon of Christian eschatology to socio-political concerns more historically than Pannenberg allows (and more directly than Schillebeeckx considers).

2. Although the point has been overstated, Pannenberg does not accord the cross of Christ the decisive, substantive role required in Christian theology. The fault lies partly in the structure of the presentation in *Jesus—God and Man,* but the problem also issues, as Pannenberg himself acknowledges, from his failure to discuss the action of God in the crucifixion of Jesus.[45] Yet Pannenberg's interpretation of the death of Jesus in terms of "Godforsakenness" provides a promising point of departure of experiential and theological significance, as Moltmann elaborates in *The Crucified God.* (a) Beyond the reversal of the judgment of the cross in Jesus' resurrection, the cross of Christ modified the resurrection in the midst of the suffering of this world, changing a future event of eschatological consummation into a present event of liberating love. Moltmann says: "Through his [Godforsaken] death the risen Christ introduces the coming reign of God into the godless present by means of representative suffering."[46] The coming Kingdom of God has taken the form of the cross in the brokenness of this world. Pannenberg has used apocalyptic effectively to develop a theological conception of universal history "broken open from the inside," but he has neglected the vibrant apocalyptic concern for the righteousness of God in history—perhaps because of the theodicy problem. All questions of theodicy aside, however, the *crucifixion* of the risen Christ can nurture Christian eschatological hope in the tragic history

---

[44]Jürgen Moltmann, *The Crucified God,* trans. R. A. Wilson and John Bowden (New York: Harper & Row, 1974) 136-45.

[45]Pannenberg, "Afterword to the Fifth German Edition," *Jesus—God and Man* (1977) 405. See Pannenberg, "Postscript," *The Theology of Wolfhart Pannenberg,* by E. Frank Tupper (Philadelphia: The Westminster Press, 1973) 305.

[46]Moltmann, *The Crucified God,* 185.

of the suffering of the world. (b) Given Pannenberg's historical and theological interpretation of Jesus' death in terms of Godforsakenness, his failure to
address the question of the suffering of God in the cross of Christ is rather
baffling. The representative character of the suffering of Christ is certainly
not contrary to the affirmation of the suffering of God. Indeed, Pannenberg's
understanding of the Trinity would seem to move him toward his own distinctive affirmation of God's suffering. Whether or not God participates in
the radical suffering of human history is a question increasingly relevant to
eschatological hope.

3. Since the affirmation of Jesus' resurrection *from* the dead makes sense
only in the eschatological horizon of the resurrection *of* the dead—which refers the issue of Jesus' resurrection to eschatological verification—Pannenberg's critics question the appropriateness of the category "historical event"
(however delimited) to characterize Jesus' destiny. Because the resurrection
of Jesus speaks the language of promise instead of the language of facts,
Moltmann considers it an eschatological event inaccessible to historical-critical judgment. He calls the resurrection a "promise event."[47] Nevertheless,
Moltmann's reconstruction does not seem very different from Pannenberg's:
(a) their faith shattered with Jesus' crucifixion, the disciples fled to Galilee;
(b) Jesus made appearances to the disciples, a revelatory "seeing" of Jesus
in the structure of anticipatory visions which included a call to mission; (c)
despite the danger they returned to Jerusalem and learned the stories of the
empty tomb.[48] Like Pannenberg, Moltmann grounds the Easter faith on the
Easter event. For Pannenberg in particular the issue of the claim of Jesus' resurrection hinges on the actuality of the appearances. Perhaps it would be
helpful to distinguish the historical character of the *assertion* of Jesus' resurrection (which constitutes an historical claim subject to historical investigation) from the metahistorical character of the *affirmation* of Jesus'
resurrection (which constitutes a faith statement subject to eschatological
verification). Of course, even this relative distinction presupposes the priority of the appearances for knowledge of Jesus' resurrection. The question of
the historicity of the resurrection heightens the issue of the appearances and
surfaces a difficult problem, namely, the subjective element in the disciples'
Easter experience.

4. Pannenberg has characterized the mode of the appearances of Jesus as
extraordinary visions, which essentially requires the event of the resurrection
of Jesus on the one side and the initiative of the risen Jesus on the other. However, because all the witnesses to the appearances of the crucified-but-risen

---

[47]Ibid., 173.

[48]Ibid., 166-68.

One are believers, Schillebeeckx (among others) faults Pannenberg for ignoring that "a faith-motivated interpretation enters into the very heart of the event."[49] Indeed, Pannenberg has not given extensive attention to the subjective element in the disciples' Easter experience, but Schillebeeckx ignores what he does say: Their faith almost destroyed by the crisis of Jesus' death, the disciples did not have the psychological resources to begin to produce confirmatory Easter experiences. Likewise, they did not have any ready-made categories from the history-of-traditions generally nor the ministry of Jesus specifically to begin to stimulate an interpretative Easter faith.[50] Pannenberg acknowledges the subjective element in other suggestions: (a) The disciples dramatically modified the apocalyptic expectation of the resurrection of the dead in using the category of resurrection to name Jesus' singular destiny in the ongoing movement of history, "something new." (b) The term "vision" expresses something about the subjective mode of the experience but nothing about the reality of the subject experienced therein. Resurrection and appearances preceded seeing and vision. (c) The disciples' inference from the appearances to the resurrection had an inner necessity: Jesus has been transformed into another mode of life. Pannenberg argues for a *faith-evoking* experience, *not* a *faith-motivated* interpretation. The subjective element which must be preserved would be: the appearances were not coercive (which would force faith). Either the appearances occurred to some who did not respond in faith, or Jesus appeared only to those who would be open to the reality of such an experience. Nevertheless, Pannenberg would do well to concede that a subjective element inheres in the New Testament witnesses to the resurrection of Jesus, a subjective element which nonetheless must be differentiated from the subjective side of any contemporary judgment about whether or not it happened.

THE DEATH AND RESURRECTION OF JESUS:
EDWARD SCHILLEBEECKX

Edward Schillebeeckx, the Dutch Roman Catholic theologian, published his massive *Jesus: An Experiment in Christology* in 1974, a decade after Pannenberg's *Jesus—God and Man*. Schillebeeckx interprets the resurrection of Jesus on the basis of "a Jewish conversion model"—in distinction from Pannenberg's eschatological model on the one side and from Bultmannian existentialist models on the other. Although Schillebeeckx's argument is quite extensive and complex, some specific points of his proposal are pivotal.

---

[49]Edward Schillebeeckx, *Jesus: An Experiment in Christology*, trans. Hubert Hoskins (New York: Seabury Press, 1979) 710n119.

[50]Pannenberg, *Jesus—God and Man*, 96.

1. With a breath-taking analysis of the various dimensions of the "good news" of Jesus Christ in the multiple Gospel traditions, Schillebeeckx considers Jesus' *Abba*-experience the secret of his life[51] and "the eschatological prophet" the crux of his identity.[52] The cheerful *good news* of the Kingdom of God constituted Jesus' central message, "with the emphasis at once on its coming and its coming close."[53] Schillebeeckx distinguishes two aspects of the single concept of *basileia:* God's rule "points to the dynamic, here-and-now character of God's exercise of control," while God's Kingdom "refers more to the definitive state of 'final good' to which God's saving activity is directed."[54] The present and future are essentially interrelated, but the accent falls on the present rule of God. Though Jesus proclaimed the imminent arrival of God's rule, nowhere does he identify this coming, "this drawing near, with the end of the world."[55] The proclamation of Jesus must be distinguished from the apocalyptic expectation of John the Baptist as well as the eschatological expectation of the early church for the parousia of Christ. Jesus united the eschatological hope for the Kingdom of God with the celebration of a new mode of conduct in the world, an orthopraxis based on the radical trustworthiness of God. Jesus was concerned with the potential for the future in the "now" of *metanoia*. Without eliminating the connection between Jesus' message and the horizon of eschatological expectation, Schillebeeckx guards the activity of Jesus on behalf of God's approaching Kingdom from the requirement of future eschatological confirmation.

2. Unlike those who see discontinuity between the death of Jesus on the one side and the church's proclamation of the resurrection of Jesus on the other, Schillebeeckx locates the "breakage-point" within the ministry of the historical Jesus, that is, the failure of his mission in Galilee and his death in Jerusalem.[56] Jesus himself had to face the task of integrating the increasing certainty of his own violent death with the will of God and of reconciling such a death with his message of the approaching Kingdom of God. Since Jesus most probably understood himself as the eschatological prophet, "he was personally confronted by reason of his approaching death with Israel's rejection of God's last offer of salvation to that people."[57] Beyond the simple acceptance of his death Jesus integrated his death with his mission of salvation,

---

[51]Schillebeeckx, *Jesus,* 256-59; but see 652ff.

[52]Note ibid., 475-80; but see 245, 306, 497.

[53]Ibid., 140.

[54]Ibid., 146.

[55]Ibid., 152.

[56]Ibid., 294-98.

[57]Ibid., 306.

a service which his very death now substantiates. At the Last Supper he acted to prepare his disciples for the shock of his death so that afterwards they would not fall into complete despair. More than farewell, the meal occasioned Jesus' offer of the prospect of renewed fellowship in the Kingdom of God after his death. So at the Last Supper Jesus passed the cup to his friends and continued to offer them a saving fellowship with him ''in spite of'' his approaching death. He said to them with this ''veiled sign'' that *''fellowship with Jesus is stronger than death.''*[58] That Jesus already understood his death as part and parcel of his mission is important, for it means that even prior to Easter Jesus communicated to the disciples that the ''Jesus affair'' will continue. The continuation is not just a vision born of faith and based solely on the disciples' Easter experience; rather, Jesus' self-understanding created the possibility and laid the foundation of the Easter interpretation of the disciples. Schillebeeckx insists: ''There is no gap between Jesus' self-understanding and the Christ proclaimed by the Church.'' The disciples could not have grasped what Jesus meant prior to the whole event of Easter. ''But after the first shock of his dying,'' Schillebeeckx reasons, ''the memory of Jesus' life and especially the Last Supper must have played a vital role in the *process* of their conversion to faith in Jesus as the Christ, the one imbued to the full with God's Spirit.''[59]

All the parties in the Sanhedrin had fundamental objections to Jesus, but they could not achieve consensus about Jesus' condemnation under the Law. The Sanhedrin finally disowned Jesus because of his silence. Since Jesus knew himself to be sent directly from God to summon Israel to faith in God, he refused to submit his mission to the doctrinal authority of the Jewish court. This contempt for Israel's highest authority constituted the Jewish legal ground for Jesus' condemnation. Though some doubts persisted about the condemnation of Jesus to death on the basis of Deuteronomy 17:12, the Sanhedrin overcame its own lack of unanimity and decided to hand Jesus over to the Romans who executed him for alleged political reasons.

Schillebeeckx concedes that Jesus' death put a severe strain on his message of the gracious nearness of the rule of God, and indeed, on Jesus himself: ''As a fact of history it can hardly be denied that Jesus was subject to an inner conflict between his consciousness of his mission and the utter silence of the One whom he was accustomed to call Father.''[60] The struggles in Gethsemane must not be cogitated out of existence, and only the loud cry at his death on the cross can be historically warranted. Nevertheless, Schillebeeckx flatly rejects the possibility that Jesus died abandoned by God. The Marcan

---

[58]Ibid., 310. Italics not in original.

[59]Ibid., 312. Italics not in original.

[60]Ibid., 317.

word—''My God, my God, why hast thou forsaken me''—evoked a reminder of all of Psalm 22: the conviction of salvation through God's nearness in this dark night of faith. ''In grief, but willingly, [Jesus] nevertheless *entrusted all his failure to God.''*[61] In his death on the cross—''the moment also of God's silence''[62]—Jesus remained faithful to God.

3. Schillebeeckx locates the question of the emergence of Easter faith in the transformation of the disciples after Jesus' death, a process of conversion that lies between two historically accessible elements.

> On the one hand, the group of disciples disintegrates because they have betrayed the very thing that keeps them together, the person of Jesus; on the other hand, reassembled in Jesus' name they proclaim, a while after Jesus' death, that this same Jesus has risen.[63]

While something must have happened, the primary and immediate response cannot be the reality of the resurrection (an eschatological eventuality not recounted in the New Testament) nor the traditions of appearances and an empty tomb (Easter faith preceded the emergence of these traditions). Instead, Schillebeeckx argues for ''a conversion process.'' After the arrest and condemnation of Jesus, the shocked disciples defected to Galilee, giving up the attempt to ''follow after Jesus.'' In a state of panic they deserted him, and they later felt their faltering to have been a failure of faith. Yet they still knew themselves to be in the merciful hands of God—something they had learned from Jesus. They had failed, but they did not undergo a complete lapse of faith. They remembered Jesus' message of God's coming rule, the forgiveness and mercy of God to those in distress, the invitation to sinners in shared meals, the promise of Jesus at his farewell meal: these memories of Jesus and their life with Jesus proved to be crucial elements in the process of conversion.[64] Because they had failed, the first condition for the conversion of the disciples would be the experience of forgiveness. Through their memory of Jesus and repentance for deserting him, Jesus renewed for them the offer of salvation. Schillebecckx says:

> In their experience here and now of ''returning to Jesus,'' in the renewal of their own life they encounter in the present the grace of Jesus' forgiving; in doing so they experience Jesus as the one who is alive. *A dead man does not proffer forgiveness.* A present fellowship with Jesus is thus restored.[65]

---

[61]Edward Schillebeeckx, *Christ: The Experience of Jesus as Lord,* trans. John Bowden (New York: Seabury Press, 1980) 825, but in the context of 824-25.

[62]Schillebeeckx, *Jesus,* 643.

[63]Ibid., 380.

[64]Ibid., 382.

[65]Ibid., 391. Italics not in original.

The experience of forgiveness, an experience illuminated by the memory Jesus' activity, constituted the matrix in which faith in the risen One occurred.

Schillebeeckx uses the model of the Jewish conversion vision to explain how the Easter experiences took the form of the Christian resurrection vision.

> In the Jewish conversion stories the conversion of a Gentile to the Jewish Law is often caled an illumination and is represented by what has become the classic model of a ''conversion vision''; the individual concerned is suddenly confronted with a brilliant light and hears a voice. . . .[66]

On the basis of the contemporary Jewish tradition of conversion by way of illumination, of enlightenment, of divine disclosure (frequently pictured in a light vision), the disciples articulated their Easter experiences in the form of resurrection appearances. Schillebeeckx concludes: ''What happens in the Christian resurrection vision (the Easter appearances) is a conversion to Jesus as the Christ, who now comes as the light of the world.''[67] The Easter experience, the recognition and acknowledgement of Jesus in the totality of his life, is only possible after his death, at the same time a recollective but new seeing of Jesus. Although it was faith motivated, the Easter experience was not just subjective; the objective, free initiative of Jesus led the disciples on to christological faith. The Easter experience is a Christian interpretation of the pre-Easter Jesus, but it is also undergirded by new experiences after Jesus' death.[68]

4. In light of the Easter experience articulated through the Christian resurrection vision Schillebeeckx examines the New Testament traditions of the ''holy sepulchre'' and the ''appearances of Christ.'' He offers notable interpretations. (a) The story of the empty tomb constitutes a negative symbol of the mystery of Jesus' resurrection in the cultic celebration of the Jerusalem church and subsequently in Mark's Gospel; however, the question of the antiquity of the tradition exposes another problem: Is it the tradition of an ''empty'' tomb or a tradition of the ''holy tomb''?[69] (b) Some women disciples, especially Mary Magdalene, first spread the report that Jesus had risen. Indeed, partly because of the experiences of these women the whole Jesus affair got started. The appearance to Mary reflects the new experience of communication and fellowship with Jesus after his death. Schillebeeckx suggests: ''Mary Magdalene may have played a part we do not know about in helping to convince the disciples that the new orientation of living which this Jesus has brought about in their lives has not been rendered meaningless by

---

[66]Ibid., 383.

[67]Ibid., 384.

[68]Ibid., 392-94.

[69]Ibid., 334-37; but see esp. 703n32.

his death—quite the opposite.''[70] (c) Apart from appearances to these women, Simon Peter was the first disciple to reach the point of conversion and to resume ''following after Jesus.'' As the first to experience what the New Testament calls ''seeing Jesus'' after his death, he took the initiative in reassembling the Twelve.[71] Schillebeeckx offers an explanatory proposal through the question:

> May it not be that Simon Peter—and indeed the Twelve—arrived via their concrete experience of forgiveness after Jesus' death, encountered as grace and discussed among themselves (as they remembered Jesus' sayings about, among other things, the gracious God) at the ''evidence for belief'': the Lord is alive?[72]

(d) The three different accounts of Paul's conversion in Acts illustrate the development of a conversion vision into an Easter appearance. The ''seeing of Jesus'' is a christological seeing, an understanding of Jesus as the Christ, but this was not called an ''official'' appearance of Christ comparable to that of Peter and the Twelve until it constituted the basis of an apostolic mission.[73]

5. In a brief addition to the third Dutch edition of *Jesus,* Schillebeeckx explicitly disassociates himself from existentialist interpretation of Rudolf Bultmann and Willi Marxsen. Against objectivist and subjectivist interpretations of Jesus' resurrection, he emphasizes the essential interdependency of the objective and subjective aspects of the apostolic belief in resurrection: ''Apart from the faith-motivated experience it is not possible to speak meaningfully about Jesus' resurrection.'' But he adds: ''Without being identical with it, the resurrection of Jesus—that is, what happened to him personally, after his death—is inseparable from the Easter experience, or faith-motivated experience, of the disciples.'' He insists:

> But besides this subjective aspect it is equally apparent that (according to Christian conviction) no Easter experience of renewed life was possible without the personal resurrection of Jesus—in the sense that Jesus' personal-cum-bodily resurrection (in keeping with a logical and ontological priority; a chronological priority is not the point here) ''precedes'' any faith motivated experience.[74]

That Jesus has risen only ''in the kerygma'' or ''in our experience as believers'' but he himself lingers ''in the realm of the dead'' is an interpretation Schillebeeckx explicitly repudiates. Nevertheless, one faith-motivated con-

---

[70]Ibid., 345.

[71]Ibid., 388-90; but see 352-60.

[72]Ibid., 391.

[73]Ibid., 360-79, esp. 378.

[74]Ibid., 645.

viction cannot legitimate another, because real legitimation remains totally eschatological. Thus Christian faith in the resurrection remains a promise for the world to come, "unsheltered and unprotected, defenseless and vulnerable." The life of the Christian is not visibly "justified" by the facts of history, but risks receiving the vindication where Jesus did: "beyond death."[75] Because of the intrinsic relation between the risen Jesus and the faith-motivated experience of the Christian community, the way the disciples came to faith in the crucified and risen One is not so different from the way Christians do so today. "So for all Christians the affirmation of their belief that God has raised Jesus from the dead may fairly describe an immediate experience of reality. . . . "[76]

6. Schillebeeckx expresses considerable reserve regarding any specific eschatological proposal. Even Jesus did not act from a well-defined concept of eschatological salvation. "Rather, he saw a distant vision of final, perfect and universal salvation—the kingdom of God—*in and through* his own *fragmentary actions,* which were historical and thus limited or finite, 'going around going good' through healing, liberating from demonic powers, and reconciliation."[77] Perspective on final salvation comes only in historically broken situations of experiences of meaning and meaninglessness, the awareness of ultimate salvation always a "negative awareness." Experiences of meaning, of love and joy, stimulate the positive formulation of conceptions of perfect salvation. However, in the history of human suffering such conceptions can only be expressed in visions and parables. What God has prepared for those who love him cannot be defined (1 Corinthians 2:9). Yet eschatological salvation does not detach persons from history but turns them toward the liberating activity of God in the world. Although the creativity of God's grace resists the presumptuous attempt to provide a fixed content to final salvation, theology does not have to remain speechless. Rather, Schillebeeckx concludes: "Faith in the risen Jesus gives us quite a *clear* perspective and not an indefinite one. Precisely here the man Jesus is the revelation of what is possible with God."[78]

Schillebeeckx offers a most provocative and cogent "experiment in christology" for contemporary theological discussion. Though not a post-Bultmannian, his interpretation inevitably invites comparison with that view. Like the students of Bultmann, Schillebeeckx interprets the Easter experience in terms of the transformation of the disciples, a faith-motivated expe-

---

[75]Ibid., 643.

[76]Ibid., 647.

[77]Schillebeeckx, *Christ,* 791.

[78]Ibid., 793.

rience. Unlike the post-Bultmannians, however, he affirms the reality of the resurrection of Jesus in conjunction with these experiences. Several intrinsic problems undermine his proposal at crucial junctures.

1. Schillebeeckx presents an oftentimes fascinating examination of the various aspects of the ministry of Jesus, eminently significant for christology and contemporary Christian ethics. However, the distinction he draws between God's rule and God's Kingdom as distinctive aspects of *basileia* is essentially artificial, designed to establish the validity of Jesus' proclamation apart from the horizon of eschatological confirmation. Not without insight Schillebeeckx locates *a* "breakage-point" in the Jesus affair between the "failure" of Jesus' mission in Galilee and the inevitability of his death in Jerusalem; nevertheless, he frames the break too narrowly and resolves it too quickly: It is one thing to say that Jesus understood his death as part and parcel of the salvation offered by God and actively incorporated his death into his mission, but it is quite another to claim that at the Last Supper Jesus assured the disciples of continued fellowship with him immediately beyond his death. Schillebeeckx solves the problem of Jesus' approach to his death too easily and too comprehensively. Does the death of Jesus not constitute a significant break with the content of his mission (as the ordeal in Gethsemane indicates)? Does the resurrection not constitute a distinctive event in the story of Jesus on the other side of the cross?

2. Despite his awareness of "the Job problem of history"—of calamity, pain and misery, of hopes unfilled—Schillebeeckx's interpretation of Jesus' struggles in Gethsemane and agony in crucifixion "cogitates" these ordeals out of the particularity of Jesus' own existence. Since the failure of Jesus' mission and the service of his death have already been integrated together in Jesus' own mind, Schillebeeckx dramatically mitigates the pathos of Jesus' passion. His interpretation of Jesus' death in terms of "the silence of God" is not inaccurate so much as inadequate. If the Abba-experience is the secret of Jesus' life and the key to his lived-out identity as the eschatological prophet, should not Schillebeeckx say something more? Schillebeeckx's preference for the concept of the silence of God at the cross not only presupposes his earlier conclusion that Jesus interpreted his death positively as a final service to God which would not end his mission (the Jesus affair) but also partly conceals another theological agenda, namely the rejection of the suffering of God, the continuing identification of Jesus with the cause of God "without contaminating God himself by his own suffering."[79]

3. The affirmation of the Easter faith prior to and apart from the appearances (and the [empty?] tomb) locates the reality of Jesus' resurrection too

---

[79]Schillebeeckx, *Jesus,* 651.

one-sidedly in the subjectivity of the disciples' experience. The initiative of Jesus in the disciples' Easter experience actually originates before the cross at the Last Supper with his "veiled promise" of fellowship with him continuing after his death. Beyond the inventive initiative of Jesus at the Last Supper, Schillebeeckx's use of the conversion model assumes that the execution of Jesus had shocked the disciples only temporarily but had not fundamentally shaken the foundation of their faith—which relates the conversion experience too heavily on their memory of Jesus and the continuing strength of their faith. Even though Schillebeeckx affirms the actuality of Jesus' resurrection, the affirmation is so bound up with the disciples' appropriation of the memory of Jesus that the meaning of resurrection for Jesus himself lacks content. In this context what does "resurrection" mean? Despite his protests, Schillebeeckx's rendering of the emergence of the Easter *kerygma* is strikingly similar to Wllli Marxsen and the post-Bultmannians. The conversion process is the externalization of the disciples' developmental experience of "seeing Jesus Christologically" which takes the form of "appearances."[80]

In addition, the use of the Jewish conversion model for interpreting the Christian resurrection vision contains several other problems: (a) The widespread availability in the first century of the Jewish conversion vision for adaptation by the disciples is historically questionable. Schillebeeckx is unable to demonstrate that this is indeed a first century model sufficiently contemporaneous with the time of Jesus and readily available to disciples to articulate the Easter experience. (b) The Jewish conversion model lacks an eschatological horizon, which the renewal of fellowship with Jesus after his death seems in some sense to presuppose. Or is resurrection a category exchangeable, for example, with the renewal of life? (c) The disciples' experience of forgiveness does not seem to demand the active presence of Jesus as much as the living memory of Jesus. Does the encounter with grace in the experience of forgiveness require any more than the recognition of the true identity and significance of the pre-Easter Jesus? (d) The relationship of the tradition of the empty tomb to the women's conversion experience remains notoriously ambiguous. If Mary experienced the first resurrection appearance in conjunction with a visit to the tomb—whether the corpse of Jesus lay within or not—how does the Jerusalem church come to the annual celebration of Jesus' resurrection at an empty tomb? (e) The interpretation of 1 Corinthians 15:1-11 as a list of *authorities* who all proclaim the same thing rather than a

---

[80]Ibid., 424-29, esp. 427-28, where Schillebeeckx concludes: "The association of the tradition of the (messianic) divine miracle-man with that of Jesus' resurrection yields the theme of 'appearances,' that is, a theologoumenon, in which Christians from an 'epiphany' tradition assimilated the resurrection kerygma from other local Christian communities, incorporating and articulating it in their own 'epiphany' theology."

list of *witnesses* to Jesus' resurrection[81] is, Schillebeeckx admits, an inter-pretation of the appearances that "constitutes a break with a centuries-old hermeneutical tradition."[82] Does Paul's claim in 1 Corinthians 15 correspond to a conversion process, and are the three accounts in Acts an illustration of the development of a conversion vision into an official Easter appearance?

4. The New Testament traditions are the only sources of contemporary knowledge of Jesus, and certainly not disinterested but faith-motivated sources. Yet Schillebeeckx minimizes the unique significance of the apos-tolic witnesses to Jesus' resurrection for later generations of Christian believ-ers. The question of Jesus' resurrection refers inevitably to the witness of the apostles—as Schillebeeckx's own analysis implies. Nevertheless, historic Christian experience cannot duplicate or reenact the original experience of the disciples who had known the historical Jesus. While the contemporary affirmation of Jesus' resurrection is a faith decision, it cannot be isolated from historical judgments about the unprecedented claim of the Easter message. The charge—"Only we suffer from the crude and naive realism of what 'ap-pearances of Jesus' came to be in later tradition, through unfamiliarity with the distinctive character of the Jewish-biblical way of speaking"[83]—is un-founded. The claim—the "belief that God has raised Jesus from the dead may fairly describe an immediate experience of reality, and not a secondary interpretation"[84]—is far from self-evident. The Easter experience of the dis-ciples depended upon the Easter event, however problematic the affirmation of eventness may turn out to be; and the naming of contemporary Christian experience refers historically to the witness of the disciples, however im-mediate such experience may be. Eschatological hope, which Schillebeeckx clearly does not intend to repudiate, requires more reliable foundations in the story of Jesus than Schillebeeckx himself is able to provide.

CONCLUSION

Contemporary theology must recognize two interrelated but distinguish-able tasks in doing Christian eschatology: (1) the grounds for eschatological hope and (2) the contents of an eschatological vision. Although he does not ignore the first task, Dale Moody focused on the second in *The Hope of Glory*. That I have worked in this essay with the initial task should not minimize the importance or the difficulty of the latter task of making constructive escha-

---

[81]Ibid., 348.

[82]Ibid., 710n119.

[83]Ibid., 346.

[84]Ibid., 647.

tological proposals (to the contrary!). Actually I consider *The Hope of Glory* Moody's most distinctive and most profoundly creative work. The inter-weaving of the biblical traditions into a constructive eschatological vision is nothing less than brilliant, a creative exercise of theological imagination sub-tly crafted in the style of biblical exegesis. Moody does not simply string Scriptures together: he forges differing biblical traditions and Christian sym-bols into a captivating eschatological proposal, a proposal which invites questions and continuing conversation. From the constructive creativity which Moody displays in *The Hope of Glory* all his students have profited. For the insistence that theology always be done within the horizon of eschatology, I am among those most in his debt.

THE ETHICS
OF DALE MOODY

PAUL D. SIMMONS
THE SOUTHERN BAPTIST THEOLOGICAL SEMINARY
LOUISVILLE KY 40280

There is no greater responsibility nor any more difficult task than to understand adequately and represent accurately the thought of another theologian. Differences of opinion and approach add to the burden of limited understandings. Add to that the problem of being sufficiently objective in dealing with persons to whom great indebtedness and profound appreciation are felt, and the task seems nearly impossible. The topic at hand compounds the problem further: Dale Moody is not an ethicist and it seems more than a bit problematic to examine his thought in that area.

Even so, the enterprise seems both desirable and necessary. Every theologian is also an ethicist since ethics is lived theology. Any systematic theology can be analyzed for the ways in which it affects moral thought and action. The way theologians think about moral issues affects the way they do theology. Method in theology is neither greatly different from nor finally separable from method in ethics.

That Dale Moody holds strong opinions on ethical issues is obvious to all who know him. That these perspectives have served as filters or backdrops for his writings is equally apparent. Precisely how that is true is of interest as an attempt is made to analyze the ethical perspectives of a Baptist theologian who is first and foremost interested in being and living as a Christian.

THE PROBLEM OF ETHICS

The problem of ethics in Protestant theology is posed by the very nature of salvation. Evangelical theology begins in the declaration that salvation is by grace alone through faith alone. The Reformation was premised on the biblical declaration that "the righteous shall live by faith" (Habakkuk 2:4; Romans 1:7). The penitential system and the works-righteousness theology of medieval Catholicism were judged heretical and non-Christian by both Luther and Calvin based on the radical insight of biblical faith. It is what God has done for human salvation and not what people may do to be saved that is the basic affirmation of salvation by God's grace.

What then is the motive for living the moral life? Fear that no incentives were sufficient beyond the threat of hell or the promise of heaven measured by a calculus of good works drove Catholicism ever deeper into a works-oriented sacramentalism. The loveless legalism that developed along with the extraordinary institutional control of believers' lives was a predictable and now thoroughly analyzed consequence.

Luther and Calvin rightly saw the errors of Catholicism and were radically captivated by the truth of salvation by grace. But they were left with the quandary so poorly resolved by their Roman interrogators. Luther was intoxicated by grace. It was the great reality—the ultimate insight into the nature of God's action and attitude toward people and thus of human salvation. In the Schmalkald Articles, he declared that the doctrine of justification by grace alone through faith alone is the basis for "all that we teach and practice against the pope, the devil and the world."[1] He regarded works righteousness as perverse and offensive to the true nature of Christianity. The law and legalism in all its forms were odious distortions of the truth of grace. Freedom is the hallmark of the Christian's life: "His freedom is God's own freedom from rules. His love is Christ working through him. His joy is the Holy Spirit dwelling in his heart."[2]

Calvin was so captivated by the power of God's grace that he was pushed into the notion of its irresistibility. He ended by asserting that all people were the objects of God's providential action—some saved by grace, the rest damned by divine fiat. Double predestination seems more an idea designed to preserve the notions of God's freedom and sovereign power than an honest effort to exegete Scripture. He would have done well to reflect upon the moral

---

[1]Cited by William Hordern, *Living By Grace* (Philadelphia: The Westminster Press, 1975).

[2]See Luther's "Christian Liberty," in *Three Treatises* (Philadelphia: Fortress Press, 1970).

nature of God rather than to hide behind the piety that God's actions are beyond moral question.

Calvin was also left with the problem of having no theological base for speaking of God's requirement for moral living on the part of the elect. If salvation is entirely by God's election (or if perdition is the destiny of some through no fault of their own, unavoidable by any virtue of their living), why should one bother with moral behavior? Hedonism would appear to have enormous appeal to converts to such a theology. Two factors avoided that trap in Calvin's approach. One was the belief that one could not *know* finally or absolutely that one was of the elect. Lack of certitude about salvation produced a spiritual anxiety that sought assurance that one was indeed of the elect. Those "assurances" were no guarantee, of course, but lifestyle was an important sign of the internal work of the Spirit. The second factor was Calvin's stress on the importance of the law as providing definitive guidance for the Christian moral life.[3] It gives a surer understanding of God's will, and it serves as a goad or whip to keep the spiritual person from becoming a laggard.[4] This stress on law has provided a legacy to Calvin's followers that has not haunted those of Luther. These two factors worked well together to constrain the adventurous and to mobilize the serious into a force for moral rectitude.

The stress falls, therefore, not on external rules or actions but on inner dynamics and dispositions. The Christian is disposed to act as God's love is experienced but is not driven to act by external requirements (rules or laws). The Christian was set free to do what the Law required without being under the requirement of the Law as such. Freedom is not, however, to do anything one may wish—it is not antinomianism or libertinism. It is freedom to do what love requires. It is freedom from sin, death and the power of Satan.

The primary work of the Law, according to Luther, was "to increase transgressions" since it revealed the sinful and rebellious works of people that merited the wrath of God. It can never justify a person, it can only condemn. Justification is the gift of God—grace freely given and producing both an alien and a proper righteousness in the believer.

All this gave Luther's thought an attractive openness of spirit that avoided the harsh negativism that was to characterize Calvin. It also set the stage for developing a "situational" or "contextual" ethics in the sphere of personal relations. Stressing God's action instead of moral deeds tended to convey a transactionalism in which the believer is set free from ethical requirements.

Critics have been quick to point out that "imputed" righteousness tends to diminish the importance of ethical responsibility. Since one is justified apart from works, one need not take works too seriously.

---

[3]See Calvin, Book II, Chapter 8, of *The Institutes*.

[4]Calvin, Book II, Chapters 7, 12, *The Institutes*.

Wesley stressed sanctification as a corrective to the moral laxity he thought to be engendered by too much emphasis on justification by faith alone. He thus resolved the issue of the incentive to live ethically by developing the notion of Christian growth as a corollary to conversion. The righteousness of faith is basic to the new covenant in Christ. Being justified is the first step in the process of transformation toward perfection, which combines the objective work of Christ with the believer's disciplined striving. Christians are not made perfect by an act of repentance but are in need of growth in grace toward maturity. The aim is to live above sin and be so purified as not to sin.

Wesley thus overcame the problem of ethics by incorporating human actions into God's saving work. He measured the Christian life by stages or states and argued that people could fall from a state of grace to a state of sin. Apostasy was possible, not only through a rational rejection of Christianity, but also by moral laxity.

As with Calvin, a new legalism emerges in Wesley, though for very different reasons. Wesley takes seriously the changes that are to characterize the believer's inner and outward life. The net result, however, was a preoccupation with *human* actions and attitudes. The believer turns inward to discern his or her spiritual state and thus enters a new bondage—the fear of falling from grace, the anxiety of not being sanctified. The importance and greatness of God's grace are lost in the focus on the human condition.[5]

THE LIFE IN CHRIST

Moody's resolution of the problem of ethics is nearer to Wesley, though he includes emphases from both Calvin and Luther (and in that order of importance). His theological frame of reference is significantly different, however, since he bases his thought in his doctrines of God, ecclesiology, salvation and eschatology.

The beginning point for Moody is the nature of reality itself or the relation of people to God. With shades of process thought, Moody cites Tillich's notion of existentialist ontology as the philosophical model for relating human actions to the divine activity. God is not pure mind as the Aristotelians would have it, but is the power of all being or the power of all existence.[6] Our being is related to and exists within God's Being: "it is in Him that we live and move and have our being" (Acts 17:28).

---

[5]For an excellent treatment of various approaches see James M. Gustafson, *Christ and the Moral Life* (New York: Harper & Row, 1968).

[6]Dale Moody, *The Word of Truth* (Grand Rapids MI: William B. Eerdmans Publishers, 1981) 99.

Furthermore, human actions have an effect on God and his future, for God is both Being and becoming. Moody declares that God is neither static immutability nor dynamic event. God is Eternal Being who acts in freedom and is constant through all change.[7] He precedes and transcends all events; he is above but within history. The things that change are God's specific activities on behalf of people (salvation history) and the divine attitude toward people (wrath, love, and so forth). He is constant in character and will, but he incarnates his extended life in believers.

Moody accepts the idea of the dipolar nature of God without compromising his commitment to supernaturalism and the personal aspects of deity. Tillich's theology portrays God as impersonal "ground of being." Moody's God is warmly personal but majestically holy. Exodus 34:6 is the textual outline of God's attributes for Moody. God is first of all defined by holiness and secondly by love.[8] Being itself is moral Being, but God is no soft or indulgent Deity. He is sovereign Lord who shows covenant love to his people and expects covenant responsibility from them.

This ontological frame of reference is the point at which Moody deals with the problem of moral incentive. The life of the believer is *within* God—not simply a life lived over against God. God is not the external judge, viewing the believer from a distance and measuring actions for their moral merit. The believer's actions are to be incarnations of the divine presence in which and for which they live. Their actions extend the power and presence of God into the world of unbelief and, in turn, contribute to God's own Being in the world. This is the truth of the incarnation—the Son incarnates the Father as the Father incorporates the Son.

The church is the body of Christ in the world and is a living, dynamic reality. It is not an institution, but an organism—a living reality—in which all believers participate. It is related to Christ, the perfect incarnation. He is the permanent embodiment of God's revelation, while the church is the incomplete process by which his incarnation is continued.[9]

The significance of baptism is thus elevated beyond that of mere symbol. Baptism is a sign of being incorporated into the body of Christ,[10] and thus has ethical significance as the dividing line *before* the life in Christ and being identified with the body of Christ. It points to what transpires between the believer and the living God. God's presence in power and His transforming Spirit are to characterize the life of the believer. Being in Christ is not an empty

---

[7]Ibid.

[8]Ibid., 97-104.

[9]Ibid., 91.

[10]Ibid., 463.

formality—it is a living, life-transforming experience in process. Verbal declarations are important but they are no substitute for solid living.

By this measure, Moody's notion of salvation is dynamic—it is a process, an ongoing venture of active relationship of the believer to God. Rejecting Calvin's double predestination, Moody says salvation involves both grace and faith. Faith is not simply intellectual assent nor "belief" in any number of propositional statements (thus rejecting Scholasticism both Catholic and Fundamentalist). Faith is inward trust and outward confession,[11] through constant responsiveness in obedience. He insists that salvation may be considered in three tenses: past, present and future.[12] The important thing is the present process—the life of commitment in ongoing relationship.

Those who live in responsive relation to God receive the gift of eternal life. Those who reject faith choose death. People are not immortal by nature, nor do they have immortal souls. God gives life to those who live in Him[13] and to them alone. Immortality is "conditional," it is not an automatic possession. Only those who love and serve God, and who live a life "worthy of their calling" (Ephesians 4:11), will live in God's eternity. One can share the very life of God here and now by participation in the Being of God but, otherwise, one perishes by going back into nothing from which creation came. Moody thus rejects universalism on ethical grounds.[14] Reciprocity in relationship is required for one to participate in the Being of God. It is a matter of faith, not a natural process or a possession by virtue of birth into the world.[15]

Moody presents a weighty message when he declares that believers are to make their election sure. The question of whether one is saved or not is thus answered in terms of growth and constancy of faith, not by a reference to a past experience. It is "necessary to supplement faith with such evidence of growth as virtue, knowledge, self-control, steadfastness, godliness, brotherly affection, and love,"[16] if one is to reach the point where one will not fall away. Sanctification, not justification, becomes the primary emphasis for Moody. It is to be possessive, progressive, and perfected.[17] It is not enough to be set aside as "holy"; one is to grow into the maturity of Christlikeness.

---

[11]*The Word of Truth*, 310.

[12]Ibid., 311, 320.

[13]Moody, *The Letters of John* (Waco TX: Word Books, 1970) 89ff.

[14]See Moody, *The Hope of Glory* (Grand Rapids MI: William B. Eerdmans Publishers, 1964) 110.

[15]See also Moody's "The End of All Things: A Summary of Eschatology Today," unpublished paper, 2-3.

[16]*The Word of Truth*, 320.

[17]Ibid., 323.

CHRISTIAN LIVING

Questions of morality are therefore questions about Christian living and must be answered in the framework of life in the Being of God. Although no elaborate treatment of ethical problems can be found in Moody's writings, he says enough for both his method and his approach to issues to be clear.

Sexual morality, for instance, is treated in the context of the eschatological significance of the human body and the ethical significance of life in the Body of Christ. Moody considers fornication to be a heinous sin, since it contradicts the sanctification of the body.[18] Paul's polemic against prostitution in I Corinthians 6, is seen by Moody as a definitive teaching regarding all non-marital coitus. One joins the Lord in body and spirit, a union that is violated when one unites with a prostitute. Here the commandment forbidding adultery (Exodus 20:14) is connected to the problem of fornication and all other forms of non-married sexual intercourse.

So strongly does Moody feel about sexual immorality that he believes it places one's salvation in question. While discussing fornication, he reminds the reader of the conditional nature of immortality, warning that it is only those who continue in the faith who will perfect their holiness.[19] Graduate students have been dismissed from supervision because of sexual laxity and Moody felt that any minister who lapsed sexually was disqualified.

Abortion is a problem Moody deals with in the light of the biblical teaching about personhood, a theology of creation and of responsible sexuality. He shares the widespread repugnance of the sexual immorality that leads to so many unplanned pregnancies in America and the subsequent resort to elective abortion. He resists and rejects the arguments of those trying to ban all abortion *by law,* however. The reasons are simple enough: the Bible teaches that with birth and breath (Genesis 2:7) one is considered a person for purposes of the law. The notion that one is a person from the moment of conception is nowhere taught in Scripture, nor is there any prohibition of abortion.

Therapeutic abortions (those for rape, incest, fetal deformity or threat to the life and health of the woman) are plainly justifiable, according to Moody. More problematic are elective abortions. But even these cannot be legally prohibited without imposing an unbiblical and theologically problematic definition of fetal personhood. The excesses of abortion should be dealt with by encouraging the development of responsible sexual ethics, not the imposition of coercive and unbiblical laws.

---

[18]Ibid., 324.

[19]Ibid., 345.

When there is no specific guidance from Scripture, Moody relies upon an imaginative and intuitive use of theological beliefs for moral guidance. The strong and dynamic activity of the Holy Spirit in the believer's life enables one to reach decisions through faith. In the midst of ambiguity and tragedy one may decide with courage and boldness. The responsibility to decide cannot be avoided. The wisdom of decisions comes from the discernment provided by the Holy Spirit as does the strength to follow through with action on options once chosen. This is the leading of the Spirit.[20]

Decisions in bioethics often fall in the grey area of ambiguity and tragedy. But the believer is not to be immobilized and thus become helpless and hopeless. One acts in hope, in faith and love, and always in the spirit of Christ. Moody's approach to issues of life and death is light years away from the legalism and dogmatism of the right-to-life movement. He regards its approach as lacking a biblical base, even though evangelical Christians adamantly claim to be rooted in Scripture. Scholasticism and rationalism, bootlegged through Francis Schaeffer and Fundamentalism, not biblical theology, underlie the mentality of the radical right.

Homosexuality is regarded by Moody as a sexual aberration which he believes disqualifies one from inheriting the kingdom of God.[21] He believes these attitudes are reflected in such passages as Leviticus 18:22, 20:13, I Corinthians 6:9, and Romans 1, and in stories such as that of the destruction of Sodom. He does not question whether or not the Bible distinguishes between orientation and behavior, or whether all dimensions of the issue are explored. He apparently assumes that the attitude(s) expressed are sufficient to establish an absolute norm against homosexuality in all its dimensions.

He stops short of regarding homosexual acts as being in a special category of immorality that deserves the harshest condemnation. He recognizes that there are also other sins that may disqualify one from kingdom membership: theft, avarice, drunkenness, angry gossip and stealing (I Corinthians 6:10). Nowhere does the Bible isolate homosexuality for special treatment. Finally, while Moody rejects "homosexuality as an approved lifestyle," he says there is hope for the homosexual in this life and the life to come. Apparently their hope for salvation is tied either to being celibate or to becoming heterosexual.

Racism is regarded by Moody as diametrically opposed to the life in Christ. The unity of creation (Acts 17:26) and the oneness of all people in Christ (Ephesians 2:14-16; Galatians 3:28) is contradicted by the attitude that

---

[20]Dale Moody, *Spirit of the Living God* (Philadelphia: The Westminster Press, 1968) 121.

[21]See *Critical Issues: Homosexuality* (Christian Life Commission, Southern Baptist Commission, n.d.) 3.

gives moral legitimacy to racial prejudice and patterns of discrimination. Moody takes justifiable pride in having preached in numerous Black churches and having been in the home of Martin Luther King, Jr. when the great civil rights leader was still a child. Through his preaching, teaching, and personal relations Moody has testified strongly to the evil of racism. He was never amused by ethnic jokes and took offense at their telling.

On this issue, Moody does not resort to Scripture quotations, the method he uses on sexual issues. Rather, he employs the themes of oneness in creation and the unity of the Church. Again the dynamics of the body as organism are important to note. One part of the body cannot discriminate against or despise the other. Those who harbor racist assumptions (as the Klan or Nazis) are by that token excluded from the Body.

It is interesting to observe that Moody has said that there might be such a thing as Christian slavery.[22] Here he relies upon the fact that slavery existed in biblical times and was tolerated by the Patriarchs, the prophets, Jesus and the apostles. Further, Moody's dispositionalism is important to note. The inner attitude may be Christian while the structure of slavery may be accepted. One can treat a slave in a Christian way, as Paul wrote concerning Philemon.

What would not be tolerable would be the institution of slavery built on racist assumptions. Slavery in biblical times was not racist—it was an economic arrangement involving no ideology of racial superiority/inferiority. The racist basis for slavery did not appear until the seventeenth century, as Gunnar Myrdal has shown.

Liberation ethics is also given short shrift in Moody's writings. His dispositionalism permits him to employ a Lutheran-like dichotomy between the inner attitude and the external structure that gives little grounds for activistic social ethics. While he rejects in theory the split between the "social" gospel and the "simple" gospel, he is not a social activist nor is he much interested in efforts to change social structures. By "social" gospel, he means "ethics" as in the morality of upright living. Structures are tolerable even when corrupt and demeaning because of one's ability to experience liberation spiritually. Liberation, he says, is an "act by which God in Christ has set men free from the slavery of sin and for a life of love for God and others."[23] Here he sounds for all the world like Luther.

Because those who are enslaved may be "redeemed" or "liberated" by faith, it is not necessary for believers to work to eliminate slavery or unjust structures. Moody's existentialist eschatology and soteriology combine in bringing him to call liberation theology a "recent radicalism." He faults it as

---

[22]From seminar discussions.

[23]*The Word of Truth*, 332.

failing the test of academic scholarship in its emphasis on revolutionary social strategies. He is sympathetic with many of the complaints against injustice by the oppressed but he is not convinced that power politics is permissible
for Christians—again his assumptions about piety and morality determine what
he means by "ethics."

Ecological concerns emerge in Moody's writings as a corollary to his interest in cosmic eschatology, though the Christian doctrines of creation and
human stewardship are also basic. He speaks approvingly of Teilhard de
Chardin's vision of all things being brought to fulfillment in Christ, though
he is critical of Teilhard's implicit notion of evolutionary progress and his
tendency toward universalism. Turning to the Bible, Moody sees eschatology related to ecology in Genesis 2 where people are portrayed as created in
relation to earth, plants and animals. All creation is portrayed in harmonious
relation, with people given the responsibility for stewardship, that is, tending
or caring for nature for the sake of the well-being of all.

Moody is especially appreciative of Paul Santimire's *Brother Earth,* which
calls for rejecting both the "adoration of nature" and the "exploitation of
nature" approaches. The former is too romantic, the latter too anthropocen-
tric, leading to reckless despoilation of the environment. He argues for an approach that ties human well-being to environmental health and that
incorporates nature into God's plan of redemption for the earth. All of creation, not just people, is the object of God's love and cosmic purpose. As
stewards, people are to protect and preserve the earth, not exploit or despoil
its beauty and resources.

Human sin, of course, threatens the earth and often contradicts God's
purposes through the impact of technology. God's providence and will for the
future are thus placed in jeopardy by human irresponsibility. Moody is no anti-
technology Luddite. But he does believe that the combination of unrestricted,
destructive technology and human sinfulness may lead to cataclysmic consequences. The Christian hope, of course, is that human cooperation with divine providence will help to bring about "consummation," a point which he
did not elaborate.[24] The direction of his thought, however, tends to envision
God's promised future as a combination of divine providence and human effort. Even earth is to be sanctified by human effort and God's grace.

War and violence also threaten the future of creation, as the nuclear crisis
shows. Moody is not a pacifist. He accepts violence as a reality on the human
scene and believes that war is here to stay: "there shall be wars and rumors
of war. . . . " In this area, Moody not only cites biblical evidences of war
and violence but also reasons from the nature of God whose holiness includes

---

[24]See "The End . . . ," 16, 17.

wrath against all ungodliness.[25] What God does cannot be immoral for people to do—that is a moral axiom for Moody. Christians may use violence when justice or right is at stake.

But there is no justification for religious zealotry as the basis of war. The *jihad* or holy war found in Islam and Judaism is a fanaticism based on a belief in the holiness of God without love.[26] Religious wars (crusades) and the persecution of people for religious beliefs (Inquisition) have no place in Christian ethics, although the mentality can be found in Christian history and currently in the New Right in religion among militant fundamentalists. Using violence against religious or theological antagonists confuses the sword of power politics with the sword of truth. God's truth is preserved by the proclaimed word and affirmed by voluntary belief. Neither coercion nor persecution have any place in the witness of the Gospel.

CONCLUSIONS AND RESPONSE

Professor Moody faithfully struggles with one of the profound problems plaguing Christianity, namely, how to conceptualize Christian moral responsibility. What are the differences that being a Christian should make? Ignorance and indifference among Christians to the moral demands of following Christ have contributed to the sorrows of the world. Some of the best arguments for atheism can be constructed by examining the history of moral blindness among Christians: the brutalities of the Inquisition, the zealotism of the Crusades, the genocide of the Holocaust, the racism of slavery and the pervasive presence of racial discrimination, the economic corruption of public Christianity, the perverse use of power by persuasive but unscrupulous hucksters, the sexual looseness of prominent ministers, are all evidences of the problem. Even those most serious about morality seem guilty of some of the most perverse notions about ethics: Luther's polemics against the Jews and his advice about the treatment of the peasants' revolt, not to mention Calvin's consent to burning Servetus, all show a perversity not consistent with the mind of Christ. The truth of God in Christ is contradicted in all these ways and more. Christianity faces a crisis of integrity when measured by the Christ of God.

Tying ethics to the very nature of being Christian is basic. Moody's method involves bringing together several elements: theological beliefs, biblical rules and instructions, central models or imaginative constructs, loyal-

---

[25]*The Word of Truth*, 97.

[26]Ibid., 96.

ties and commitments, and an evaluation of data.[27] Philosophical underpinnings are found in personalism, existentialist ontology and process thought. Moody's commitment to the Bible is the frame of reference in which he operates, even though assumptions are often made that tend to result in problematic understandings of certain passages. His broad grasp of and acquaintance with theological traditions and his knowledge of a broad range of subjects is both intimidating and admirable. He has been less successful in bringing together his own ethical method in a systematic and cohesive fashion that altogether satisfies the demands of his own aspirations.

Tying the notion of apostasy to the possibility of moral lapses by the Christian both underscores the importance of moral living and lapses into legalism. Following Wesley at this point has the salutary effect of reminding Christians of the importance of growth in the Christian life and bringing sanctification into focus along with justification. But it also tends to diminish the importance of salvation by grace. In the final analysis even Christian growth is the gift of grace not simply the end product of personal striving. All of life and love and wholeness are the gift of God.

At least part of the problem in Moody's thought is found in his doctrine of God. The first feature of God is "holiness," according to Moody, which makes good Hebrew theology but not good *Christian* theology. His holiness involves wrath, righteousness and power among other things.[28] The second major feature of God is love, which Moody does admit as "the high point in the biblical portrayal of God."[29] As loving, God can be spoken of as mercy, grace, patience, and so on, following Exodus 34:6. One would have thought that Moody would have worked out his theology of Being in terms of an ontology of love if he is serious about beginning with the supreme revelation of God which was in Christ. For Jesus, the two great words were *abba* and *agape*—an open challenge to the priestly notions of Holiness and Otherness.

Moody's notion of God is a corollary to his approach to apostasy. Salvation is not assured except for the morally upright—and who are they? Like Calvin and Wesley, Moody leaves believers more than a bit nervous—anxious about a salvation which is never quite sure. Nervous Nellies make energetic workers in church and society, embracing in practice what Weber called the Protestant ethic. Their "drivenness" is often a type of workaholism, as Wayne Oates argues. Beneath all that striving seems the fear that one is not acceptable. The unconscious effort seems to be to achieve salvation, to

---

[27]For helpful approaches to method in ethics see the chapters by Page Lee and Glen Stassen in *Issues in Christian Ethics* edited by Paul D. Simmons (Nashville TN: Broadman Press, 1980).

[28]*The Word of Truth*, 97.

[29]Ibid., 104.

prove oneself acceptable to God and others—and to be loved. The haunting fear is that one is rejected, a castaway, and the desire is to show that one is truly righteous, a good person deserving favor.

Moody rightly rejects Calvin's double predestinarianism recognizing the reciprocity of grace and faith. But he leaves us with the Wesleyan quandary—who is really saved? The result is still a mysterious shell game between God and the believer.

A further part of the problem can be seen in the influence of covenant theology which Moody holds.[30] Christians are given helpful moral guidance by the law and commandments of Scripture. These form stipulations and requirements for parties to the agreement. The model of covenant is juridical, following Calvin, not primarily relational or personal. As Brunner showed, one can appreciate the value of guidance without substituting a requirement of law for the immediacy of response in the freedom of grace.

Calvin's legalistic influence shines through Moody's approach to sexual ethics perhaps more clearly than in other areas. Sexual matters are a top priority in Moody's thought. Even his comments about the dangers of "the flesh,"[31] seem narrowly construed as sexual temptation rather than as a way of life that disregards the lordship of Christ. Sexual misconduct is not all that is involved in living by the flesh. Thus, in spite of his polemics against legalism, Moody betrays a Puritan suspicion about sex and seems to judge salvation too readily where sexual misconduct is concerned. His fears about sexual matters apparently figure in his reluctance truly to hear Paul's profound polemic against legalism in Galatians. Both antinomian hedonism and rigoristic legalism were enemies of grace, according to Paul. Those who espoused the necessity of any requirement for salvation other than God's grace "were fallen from grace." By this reading, Moody is in trouble!

Moody thus combines moral requirements (legalism) with his existentialist ontology in developing his theology of salvation. Had he developed the ontological approach he probably would have come out nearer to Daniel Day Williams[32] than to Calvin and Wesley. Believers then would not be judged by external and arbitrary rules about sex so much as they would be challenged to develop responsible sexual relations consistent with their life in the Being of God.

Another area of concern is in Moody's approach to social ethics. At many points his theology would seem to lead to great support for and compatibility

---

[30]Ibid., 108, 327.

[31]Ibid., 351.

[32]Daniel Day Williams, *The Spirit and the Forms of Love* (New York: Harper & Row, 1968).

with liberation ethics. He draws back, however, committed as he is to more pietistic measures of Christian responsibility. He spiritualizes liberation, making it an existential freedom that transcends chains, prisons and radical oppression. Not only does he not challenge the abuse of power by the tyrant who perpetuates structures of injustice, he criticizes the oppressed who are trying to challenge such structures.

In this important area, Moody seems more Lutheran than Reformed. He resorts more upon the Spirit's claims on the inner life of piety and personal love, than the claims of the God of justice for bringing society under His sovereign lordship. Moody is strong on the demands of love but has not worked out the relation of love to justice. As the liberationists point out, salvation in the Bible is related to human wholeness—bodily integrity is tied to spiritual redemption. Thus, deliverance from political tyranny and economic deprivation is also part of what God wills for his people. Salvation has important political ramifications as the Exodus shows. How can Christians claim to love when they are indifferent to the plight of the oppressed of the earth? Again, Moody's soteriology could be a powerful base from which to develop the concern for a commitment to social justice as a corollary to the incorporating and participating power of love in personal relations.

Moody's ethics then are a combination of personal pietism, covenant legalism, biblical principlism and biblical theology. As a Christian believer, Moody stands tall. He is a person of impeccable integrity and Christian conviction. His powerful intellect is matched only by his depth of warmth and genuine piety. Few people have the ability of Moody to debate with the most astute philosophical minds and weep sympathetically with the repentant and contrite. He has been a powerful influence to me and has aided my struggle more perfectly to understand the biblical materials and to systematize my own thought. My indebtedness, like my appreciation, runs deep for this giant of the faith.

Conviction is an important term for Moody. It is not simply an intellectual matter, it is also a moral matter. When God leads a believer to a position, contending for its rightness until shown otherwise by Scripture and reason becomes a moral mandate. To capitulate under pressure is to show moral cowardice—to fail in one's obedience to the Christ who stood firm, even to the cross. On this he is right though he has been criticized as being bulldog tough and uncompromising. He is a man solidly nurtured by Christian pietism and profoundly committed to the truth of God as he sees it. He is molded in this area by two powerful images. One is Luther at the Diet of Worms proclaiming against threats to life and liberty, ''Here I stand, God being my helper, I can do no other unless shown by Scripture and reason.'' The other is the Alamo. When Colonel Travis drew a line in the sand and challenged the courageous to stay, he required a commitment that both tested their resolve and required their life. Those are powerful pictures of faith in action that still fashion the lives of heroes in the faith.

DALE MOODY:
A BIBLIOGRAPHY

PAUL M. DEBUSMAN
THE SOUTHERN BAPTIST THEOLOGICAL SEMINARY
LOUISVILLE KENTUCKY 40280

[Editor's Note: This listing of the books written by Dale Moody has been abstracted from a definitive complilation of his writings by Paul M. Debusman, The Southern Baptist Theological Seminary, Louisville, KY 40280. Debusman's thiry-four page bibliography includes hundreds of items arranged in the following categories: books, contributions to books, encyclopedia and dictionary articles, journal articles, Southern Baptist curriculum, periodical and newspaper articles, non-Baptist newspaper articles, audio-visual materials, book reviews and shorter book notes, unpublished materials, and collections of materials. Obviously such a listing cannot be reproduced here but a copy is available at the Boyce Library at The Southern Baptist Theological Seminary, or the reader may write Dr. Debusman requesting further information about its availability.]

Christ and the Church: An Exposition of Ephesians with Special Application to Some Present Issues. Grand Rapids: Eerdmans, 1963.

The Hope of Glory. Grand Rapids: Eerdmans, 1964.

Baptism: Foundation for Christian Unity. Philadelphia: Westminster Press, 1967.

Spirit of the Living God: The Biblical Concepts Interpreted in Context. Philadelphia: Westminster Press, 1968.

The Letters of John. Waco TX: Word Books, 1970.

Scripture, Baptism and the Ecumenical Movement: Two Lectures. Disciples
    Institute for the Study of Christian Origins, Tübingen, 28-29 April, 1970;
    published by the European Evangelistic Society, Aurora IL

*The Word of Truth: A Summary of Christian Doctrine Based on Biblical Rev-
    elation.* Grand Rapids: Eerdmans, 1981.